Lucy Waverman's
fast & fresh cookbook

Lucy Waverman's
FAST & FRESH
cookbook

FIREFLY BOOKS

A Firefly Book

Published by Firefly Books 1997

Cataloguing-in-Publication Data

Waverman, Lucy
    Fast & fresh cookbook

Includes index.
ISBN 1-55209-106-6

1. Quick and easy cookery.   I. Title.
II. Title: Fast & fresh cookbook.

TX833.5.W38   1997   641.5'55   C96-932530-4

Design and page production: Counterpunch/Linda Gustafson & David Vereschagin

Published by
Firefly Books Ltd.
3680 Victoria Park Avenue
Willowdale, Ontario
Canada M2H 3K1

Published in the U.S. by
Firefly Books (U.S.) Inc.
P.O. Box 1338, Ellicott Station
Buffalo, New York 14205 U.S.A.

Printed and bound in Canada by Friesens, Altona, Manitoba

Printed on acid-free paper

contents

acknowledgements

I owe a large debt of gratitude to Joseph Hoare, my editor at *Toronto Life* magazine, for his support for my column, "Faster Foods." Many of the recipes in this book originally appeared in that column.

I also want to thank Marilyn Linton and Cynthia David at the *Toronto Sun* for their support and encouragement. My "Learning with Lucy" column was also a source of recipes for this book.

Shelley Tanaka has again been my invaluable editor, turning this book into a readable, workable entity.

To Claire Arfin, for once again testing and tasting.

To my husband, Bruce, who tasted, tested and always encouraged, a special thanks.

Thanks to Emma, Katie and Alex, who have paid me the great compliment of being good, creative cooks.

And to Jan Whitford, my agent, who said she never wanted to take on a cookbook, thank you.

introduction

There are several fast and furious cookbooks on the market, so why would you choose this one? If you believe that super gourmet dinners in under thirty minutes are only for supermen or superwomen in the kitchen, you and I have something in common. We ordinary mortals need a little time and energy to produce good food. This book provides the tools for people who want to cook tasty, interesting dishes but don't want to spend a lot of time in the kitchen. Many of the recipes are suitable for entertaining; this is more than a quick, family cookbook.

Despite modern time limitations, I still like to cook a quality, tasty dinner for my family. Sitting around the dinner table is the best time to exchange news and information and find out what's happening in my family's lives. This book was born out of these dinners. It will help you turn out that great dish with some simple accompaniments in record time. Some of the recipes will even enable you to put together a three-course extravaganza in under an hour.

When I have people over (and I find that more and more I'm going back to entertaining at home instead of eating out), I don't want to spend two days preparing a meal that will leave me so tired that I can't wait for the guests to leave. I prefer to cook a simple but satisfying meal that I can shop for and prepare in an afternoon – leaving me time to shower and tidy up the house.

I like well-flavoured food, and I like to use fresh seasonal ingredients when they are available (I try not to make tomato salads in the winter or root vegetable gratins in the summer). Our northern climate dictates using some canned products (such as tomatoes), and I often use canned beans (which take too long to cook from the dried state when you are in a hurry). Canned salmon and tuna can also be useful substitutes for fresh in fish patties, chowders and pasta sauces. Cooking fresh food without resorting to packaged products laced with additives and preservatives makes me feel I am contributing to the health of my family.

I believe that good meals can be produced with good results by the average cook in about an hour. I have concentrated on interesting dishes – many a little out of the ordinary – that will perk up your taste buds, without tiring you out.

I am not a trained nutritionist so this is not a nutrition book, but because of my desire to cook healthful food, I have kept the fat content reasonably low without sacrificing taste as well as suggesting that you keep salt content to a minimum by adding it to taste.

As in my other books, I have included tips, techniques and general food information where it is applicable so this book will be more than a recipe collection, but a book to read as well.

I long to be so organized that I could walk into my kitchen in the late afternoon and in a few moments put the finishing touches on a meal I have prepared the night before. Unfortunately, I'm not that well organized. Besides, I would rather spend the evenings with my family or reading – not chopping onions.

I hope this book will help you entertain friends or feed your family great meals – without having to live in your kitchen.

Lucy Waverman

chapter one

FAST COOKING BASICS

*T*here are a number of things you can do to make your life easier in the kitchen. With a little advance planning, a basic knowledge of a few simple cooking techniques, and a well-equipped store cupboard you can prepare the recipes in this book quickly and easily to feed your family interesting meals, or even entertain unexpected guests with style.

how to be a fast and fresh cook

These are the basic techniques I use to make my time in the kitchen efficient and enjoyable.

■ Make things ahead of time. Dips and spreads can be made up to three days ahead of time. All soups are as good or even better reheated. Salads can be prepared in advance but not tossed with their dressing until just before serving. Any meat, chicken or fish dish that is cooked in a liquid can be prepared up to the point of baking and then baked when needed. Vegetables can be cooked just until crisp-tender, refreshed under cold running water until they are cold, and then sautéed in a little butter and lemon or resteamed when needed. Most desserts can be made ahead, and fresh fruit salads improve with extra marinating time.

■ Make a bottle of vinaigrette and use it to dress salads all week long. As long as the dressing doesn't contain egg yolk or cream, it should last for at least one month. Cream- and yolk-based dressings should last about one week.

■ Wash and dry lettuce as soon as you bring it home (I keep several different kinds). Break the greens into bite-sized pieces and place in a plastic bag with a slice of bread to absorb any liquid (replace the bread if it gets soggy). Use the greens all week for salads.

■ Chop enough onions for a week and store them in a plastic container in the refrigerator.

■ Chop several cloves of garlic, place in a dish, cover with oil and keep in the refrigerator until needed.

■ Peel and finely chop several tablespoons of ginger root. Cover with white wine and store in a jar in the refrigerator for up to two weeks. The wine can be used in sauces.

■ Grate the rind of a couple of lemons and keep the grated rind wrapped in plastic wrap until needed. Squeeze the juice from the lemons and use in sauces, salad dressings or soups.

■ Chop a bunch of parsley and keep it covered with plastic wrap in the refrigerator. Use as an instant garnish.

■ If you make pastry, make a double batch, roll out the second batch and freeze it already in the pie plate. You are much more likely to make a pie if the pastry is already prepared.

fast cooking techniques

The "fast and fresh" cook needs to know only a few basic techniques. The following quick-cooking terms are used in this book.

Blanch – Blanching is a preliminary cooking method, where food is partially cooked by being immersed in boiling water. Blanching is used mainly for vegetables that will be incorporated into other dishes or reheated. It is also used to remove the skin of foods such as nuts or tomatoes, or to seal in juices.

Bring a large pot of water to a boil. Add the food and boil for 1 to 2 minutes. Drain and refresh the food under cold running water. If the food is to be reheated, refresh until cold; if the food is to be used immediately, refresh only to stop the cooking.

Grill – Most foods should be grilled on high heat. The intense, direct heat of the broiler or barbecue sears the food and helps to seal in the juices. (Grilling, broiling and barbecuing are essentially the same techniques.)

Lightly oil the food and place it on a baking sheet or broiler pan under a preheated broiler, or on a rack over the barbecue.

Marinate – Immersing meat in a flavoured oil and acid mix tenderizes and flavours it. Marinating can be done for a short time at room temperature, or for several hours or overnight in the refrigerator (refrigerator cold slows down the process). Delicate foods such as fish or chicken tend to lose their flavour if they are marinated for a long time.

Make sure the food is completely coated with the marinade or turn the food in the marinating dish several times. Use a flat, non-corrosive dish (you will need less marinade than if you use a bowl).

Poach – Delicate foods can be cooked gently in a liquid that is barely simmering. Foods such as fish or seafood should be poached, since more intense simmering or boiling will toughen the delicate tissues.

Bring the poaching liquid to a gentle simmer on medium-low heat. Add the food and poach until it is cooked through. The poaching liquid can sometimes be used as the basis for a sauce.

Reduce – Reducing a sauce or stock concentrates the taste by boiling off some of the water and intensifying the essential flavour of the liquid.

Place a skillet or wide pot on a stove on medium-high heat and add the liquid. Boil, uncovered, until the liquid reduces to the amount you want. Shake the pan occasionally (you can stir, but this is not necessary). The liquid should thicken slightly and take on a silky texture and sheen.

Refresh – Pouring cold water over a cooked vegetable stops the cooking and helps the vegetable retain its colour.

Run about 2 cups (500 mL) cold water over the drained vegetable if you are serving it right away, but if you are reheating it later, run cold water over until the food is cold. This will stop the cooking completely.

Sauté – Sautéing uses less fat than frying. Many vegetables and small pieces of meat, poultry or fish can be cooked by this method, which seals in juices.

Place a skillet on medium-high heat. Heat a small amount of oil or butter, then add the food. Toss with a wooden spoon or other implement until the food is cooked and slightly browned.

Stir-fry – Stir-frying is essentially the same technique as sautéing, but is traditionally an Oriental technique done in a wok, using two implements to toss the food so that it cooks quickly and evenly.

Place a wok or large skillet on the stove on the highest heat possible. Let the pan heat up until a wisp of smoke appears. Then add the oil. In Oriental dishes, flavourings such as garlic, ginger, chili peppers and green onions are usually stir-fried first. Then meat is added, followed by vegetables (cook the firmest vegetables first). Stir-fries are often finished with a seasoning/thickening sauce that consists of cornstarch, soy sauce, stock, sesame oil and other flavourings.

Add food in small batches so the temperature of the wok is not lowered too much. If necessary, remove foods from the pan as they cook, then return everything to the wok just before adding the sauce.

the store cupboard

What you have on your kitchen shelves can make or break you when you are trying to prepare a meal quickly. A well-equipped cupboard will not only stop you from having to run out to the store in the middle of a recipe, but it will also enable you to put together a tasty meal at the last minute from the staples you have on hand. Stock basic necessities but also some optional extras, which will give you more flexibility when you are choosing what to cook.

Sauces and seasonings:
Dijon mustard, ketchup, Tabasco, Worcestershire sauce, dried chili flakes, soy sauce, salt, peppercorns for the peppermill, tomato paste, dry mustard, garlic, fresh ginger, vegetable oil, olive oil, red and white wine vinegars, white vinegar, herbs and spices, orange liqueur.
Optional extras: Balsamic vinegar, fruit-flavoured vinegar, sesame oil, nut oils, Chinese chili paste, hoisin sauce.

Baking ingredients:
Baking powder, baking soda, all-purpose flour, whole wheat flour, natural bran, rolled oats, cornstarch, arrowroot, dried fruits, vanilla extract, almond extract, icing sugar, brown sugar, granulated sugar, honey, cocoa, molasses, gelatine, unsweetened chocolate, bittersweet or semisweet chocolate, corn syrup, desiccated coconut, peanut butter.

Pasta, rice, beans and grains:
Long-grain rice, short-grain rice, dried noodles (such as linguine), dried short pasta (such as penne), lentils, barley, bulgur, buckwheat, quick-cooking couscous.

Canned goods:
Salmon, tuna, jams and jellies, chicken and beef broth, canned tomatoes, pimentos, kidney beans (white and red), chickpeas, jalapeño peppers.

Refrigerator staples:
Mayonnaise, shortening, horseradish, capers, butter, margarine, fresh lemons and limes, orange juice, Parmesan cheese, sour cream, plain yogourt, maple syrup, black olives, anchovies.

chapter two

APPETIZERS & LIGHT DISHES

A beautiful tray of hors d'oeuvres or tempting first course can whet your appetite and set the mood for the meal ahead. Unfortunately, making appetizers can be fiddly and time-consuming and, when you are busy concentrating on preparing a main dish, they can seem like a waste of time.

However, appetizers don't have to take a long time to make. Many of the dishes in this chapter are quick and easy to prepare, and a number of the soups, salads, vegetable and pasta dishes throughout the book also make fast first courses. In addition, this chapter includes a number of dishes suitable for brunch, lunch or a light supper.

tips

- Many of us don't want to spend time making too many labour-intensive little bites. If you are entertaining, try making one simple dip and one more intricate hors d'oeuvre.
- If you are having an elegant dinner, don't serve too many hors d'oeuvres with drinks. One or two per person are enough. Because they are hungry, people will often graze through as many nibblies as you provide, and then they don't appreciate the rest of the meal.
- Having dips and spreads in the refrigerator takes care of friends who drop in unexpectedly. And they are great to have on hand for quick snacks. Pack the dip in a small yogourt container and take along with some vegetables and crackers for a great portable lunch.
- For a more elegant presentation, try serving dips in pretty bowls, or use hollowed-out vegetables such as cabbage, artichokes or peppers.
- Don't be restricted to crackers or carrot and celery sticks for dips. Use snow peas, green beans, broccoli and cauliflower florets and Belgian endive – either raw or cooked until crisp-tender – as well as breadsticks, Pita Toasts (recipe follows), or even cold seafood, meat and fruit.
- If you are serving a first course at the table before a special meal, make one that complements the main course. For example, don't follow a creamy appetizer with a creamy main dish, and avoid serving seafood before fish. Appetizer salads that have a main ingredient such as smoked fish or cheese are particularly good when you have a rich dish to follow.

pita toasts

These little toasts are perfect as canapé bases or for dipping into strongly flavoured dips. Spread pita breads with butter. Cut each bread into 6 triangles. Place on a buttered baking sheet and bake at 400° F (200° C) for 5 minutes, or until browned and crisp.

homemade melba toast

Trim the crusts off thinly sliced bread. Cut each slice in half. Lay on baking sheets and bake at 250° F (120° C) for 30 minutes, or until golden-brown and slightly curled.

For seasoned melba toast, rub the bread with half a clove of garlic or sprinkle with dried herbs before baking.

eggplant dip

This smoky dip is similar to the Middle Eastern eggplant dip, baba ganoush. Make it with low-fat yogourt and light mayonnaise to keep the calories down without sacrificing taste. Serve with Pita Toasts (see page 8). The dip should keep in the refrigerator for one week.

1	large eggplant	1
2	cloves garlic, peeled	2
2 tbsp	coarsely chopped parsley	25 mL
1 tbsp	lemon juice	15 mL
1 tsp	ground cumin	5 mL
½ tsp	ground coriander	2 mL
½ cup	plain yogourt	125 mL
½ cup	mayonnaise	125 mL
1 tsp	sesame oil	5 mL
	Salt and freshly ground pepper to taste	

1 Preheat the oven to 425° F (220° C).
2 Prick the eggplant in three spots and place on a baking sheet. Bake for 45 to 60 minutes, or until soft. Cool slightly. Cut in half, drain out any liquid and scoop out the flesh. There should be about 2 cups (500 mL).
3 In a food processor or blender, with the machine running, drop the garlic and parsley through the feed tube and chop finely. Add the eggplant, lemon juice, cumin and coriander. Process until smooth.
4 Add the yogourt, mayonnaise and sesame oil and combine well. Season with salt and pepper.

5 Pile the dip into a serving bowl and refrigerate, covered, until ready to serve.
Makes about 3 cups (750 mL)

greek garlic cheese spread

This earthy, lusty spread can be served as a dip with vegetables or cooked shrimp, or it can be spread on Belgian endive leaves or toast. If you are using it as a dip, thin the mixture slightly with more sour cream. The spread should keep, refrigerated, for a week.

3	cloves garlic, peeled	3
¼ cup	coarsely chopped parsley	50 mL
4	anchovies	4
¼ cup	green olives, pitted	50 mL
6 oz	feta cheese, crumbled	180 g
4 oz	cream cheese, at room temperature	125 g
½ cup	sour cream	125 mL
1 tsp	dried oregano	5 mL
¼ tsp	cayenne pepper or Tabasco	1 mL

1 In a food processor or blender, with the machine running, drop the garlic through the feed tube and chop finely. Add the parsley, anchovies, olives, feta and cream cheese and process until well combined.
2 Add the sour cream, oregano and cayenne and process until smooth.
Makes about 2 cups (500 mL)

aioli

Aioli is the magnificent garlic mayonnaise of southern France. It is sometimes called the butter of Provence because it is spread on everything, including bread, crackers and vegetables. Refrigerated, it should keep for up to five days.

For a variation, add 2 tbsp (25 mL) chopped fresh basil (or 2 tsp/10 mL dried) to turn the aioli into a lovely accompaniment to sliced tomatoes, fried eggplant or as a spread for French stick or grilled bread. Or add 2 tbsp (25 mL) chopped fresh tarragon (or 2 tsp/10 mL dried) to make a superb sauce for fried chicken or hamburgers.

3	cloves garlic, peeled	3
2	egg yolks	2
	Juice of ½ lemon	
1½ cups	olive or vegetable oil	375 mL
	Salt and freshly	
	ground pepper to taste	

1 In a food processor or blender, with the machine running, drop the garlic through the feed tube and chop it finely. Add the egg yolks and half the lemon juice and blend.
2 With the machine running, slowly drip the oil down the feed tube until it has all been absorbed. Add the remaining lemon juice and salt and pepper. If the mixture is too thick, whirl in 1 to 2 tbsp (15 to 25 mL) hot water. Refrigerate until needed.
Makes about 2 cups (500 mL)

grand aioli

The "grand" aioli makes a super summer brunch dish or light dinner on days when it is too hot to cook. Surround a bowl of aioli with a combination of leftover cooked chicken or fish, ham, hard-boiled eggs, cooked new potatoes, green beans, broccoli and carrots.

mayonnaise tips

■ Mayonnaise coagulates more easily if it is made with room-temperature eggs. If the eggs are cold, place them in a bowl of warm water for five minutes before using.
■ If your mayonnaise doesn't emulsify (the egg and oil don't mix together and the mixture looks curdled), remove the mayonnaise from the food processor or blender and add another egg yolk to the work bowl. Gradually beat the curdled mayonnaise into the egg yolk – it should re-emulsify.

cheese medley dip

I first tasted this at a lodge in Wisconsin. It was so good that I have adapted it for all sorts of uses. Spread the medley on bread or crackers, or serve it as a dip with raw vegetables. Keep some on hand to slather on a ham sandwich or melt over a steak (store it in the refrigerator, covered, for up to two weeks). It is also wonderful on potatoes or layered in a potato casserole.

½ cup	**mayonnaise**	**125 mL**
½ cup	**finely chopped fresh spinach**	**125 mL**
¼ cup	**grated Cheddar cheese**	**50 mL**
¼ cup	**grated Parmesan cheese**	**50 mL**
¼ cup	**cottage cheese**	**50 mL**
2 oz	**cream cheese, at room temperature**	**60 g**
2 tbsp	**crumbled blue cheese**	**25 mL**
1 tbsp	**finely chopped fresh basil, or 1 tsp (5 mL) dried**	**15 mL**
2	**cloves garlic, minced**	**2**
1 tsp	**Worcestershire sauce**	**5 mL**

1 Combine all the ingredients by hand or in a food processor and blend together until smooth.

Makes about 2 ½ cups (625 mL)

spicy tomato dip

Serve this with celery sticks or as a low-calorie dressing over raw vegetables such as cucumbers, celery, green onions and carrots. It should keep, refrigerated, for up to three days.

1	**clove garlic, peeled**	**1**
3 tbsp	**coarsely chopped parsley**	**45 mL**
1	**tomato, cut in half**	**1**
1 tsp	**ground coriander**	**5 mL**
1 tsp	**ground cumin**	**5 mL**
1 tsp	**dried tarragon**	**5 mL**
½ cup	**plain yogourt**	**125 mL**

1 In a food processor or blender, with the machine running, drop the garlic and parsley through the feed tube and chop finely.
2 Add the remaining ingredients and purée until smooth.

Makes ½ cup (125 mL)

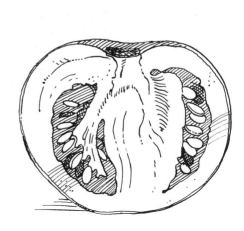

yogourt chutney dip

Serve this with fresh vegetables, cooked shrimp or Pita Toasts (see page 8). It should keep, refrigerated, for up to three days.

If you use low-fat yogourt, this dish is very low in calories.

½ cup	plain yogourt	125 mL
1 tsp	mango chutney	5 mL
1 tsp	curry powder	5 mL
2 tbsp	chopped green onions	25 mL

1 In a small bowl, combine all the ingredients.
Makes ½ cup (125 mL)

cajun seasoning

In a jar, combine 2 tbsp (25 mL) dried basil, ⅓ cup (75 mL) salt, ¼ cup (50 mL) freshly ground pepper, 2 tbsp (25 mL) cayenne pepper, 2 tbsp (25 mL) dried thyme, ⅓ cup (75 mL) paprika and ⅓ cup (75 mL) garlic powder. Shake to combine thoroughly. Cover and store in a cupboard for up to one year.

Makes about 1½ cups (375 mL)

cajun-spiced chickpeas

The ultimate nibble – spicy, high in fibre and low in fat. Because chickpeas are rather bland, use strong seasonings. Put the chickpeas in bowls and place them around the room for people to munch on. Store them in the refrigerator, covered, for up to two weeks. For a variation, use curry powder instead of the Cajun seasoning.

2 tbsp	butter	25 mL
1	clove garlic, finely chopped	1
1 tsp	Cajun seasoning, or to taste	5 mL
1 cup	drained canned chickpeas	250 mL
	Salt and freshly ground pepper to taste	

1 In a medium skillet, heat the butter on low heat. Add the garlic and Cajun seasoning. Stir together and cook for 1 minute or until the butter smells fragrant.
2 Add the chickpeas and cook, stirring occasionally, for 7 to 10 minutes, or until they have absorbed the butter and seasonings. Sprinkle with salt and pepper. Cool and serve at room temperature.
Makes 1 cup (250 mL)

easy grilled bread

Called speidini in Italy, this is a superior barbecued or broiled bread to serve as a first course or with a main course.

1	loaf French or Italian bread	1
2 cups	grated mozzarella cheese	500 mL
	(about 8 oz/250 g)	
1	2-oz (50 g) can anchovies,	1
	drained and chopped	
3	tomatoes, peeled, seeded and chopped	3
½ cup	olive oil	125 mL
1	clove garlic, minced	1
1 tbsp	chopped fresh basil, or	15 mL
	1 tsp (5 mL) dried	
¼ tsp	freshly ground pepper	1 mL

1 Cut the bread into slices 1 inch (2.5 cm) thick.
2 In a medium bowl, mix together the cheese, anchovies and tomatoes.
3 In a small bowl, combine the olive oil, garlic, basil and pepper.
4 Brush the oil mixture over both sides of the bread slices until they are well soaked.
5 Broil or barbecue the bread. Top with the cheese/anchovy mixture, pressing it down firmly. (If you are using a broiler, broil both sides of the bread before adding the topping; if you are grilling on a barbecue, grill 1 side only and spread the cheese/anchovy mixture on the toasted

side.) Continue to barbecue or broil until the cheese melts.
Serves 6 (about 2 slices each)

smoked salmon mousse

Serve this simple mousse spooned onto lettuce leaves on individual plates. Surround with cucumber slices. Alternatively, serve the mousse in a crock surrounded by hot buttered toast or crackers, and let guests help themselves. The mousse should keep for one week, covered and refrigerated.

4 oz	cream cheese,	125 g
	at room temperature	
¼ cup	whipping cream	50 mL
3 oz	smoked salmon, finely chopped	90 g
2 tbsp	finely chopped green onions	25 mL
1 tbsp	lemon juice	15 mL
pinch	cayenne pepper	pinch
	Salt and freshly	
	ground pepper to taste	

1 In a medium bowl, beat the cream cheese with the cream until light and creamy. Fold in the smoked salmon and green onions. (Or, process all ingredients in a food processor until slightly chunky.)
2 Season to taste with the lemon juice, cayenne, salt and pepper.
Serves 4

smoked trout salad

If you can, buy smoked trout on the bone, as it is more moist than trout fillets. Smoked sturgeon or smoked salmon can be substituted.

1	head Boston lettuce	1
1	whole smoked trout, or 2 fillets	1
	(about 12 oz/375 g)	
2	Belgian endives, thinly sliced	2
1 cup	finely chopped red onion	250 mL
1 cup	chopped English cucumber	250 mL

lemon walnut vinaigrette

2 tbsp	walnut oil	25 mL
2 tbsp	olive oil	25 mL
1 tbsp	lemon juice	15 mL
	Salt and freshly	
	ground pepper to taste	

1 Separate the lettuce and cover 4 serving plates with lettuce leaves.
2 Remove the skin from the trout. Slip a knife between the flesh and bones and ease off the fillets. Separate the fish into bite-sized pieces and pile on top of the lettuce.
3 Scatter the endive, onion and cucumber over each serving.
4 In a small bowl, whisk together the vinaigrette ingredients. Drizzle the vinaigrette over the salad before serving.
Serves 4

english cucumbers

Long English cucumbers are crisp, tasty and worth the extra cost because they have no seeds. Look for a dark-green skin without any yellow patches, and avoid puffy or soft ones. Wrap the cucumbers in plastic wrap after cutting and refrigerate. They should keep for about one week.

charred tuna carpaccio

A fast way to produce a wonderfully tasty dish that is good served hot or cold. The fish should be charred on the outside and pink in the middle.

½ tsp	dried rosemary	2 mL
½ tsp	dried thyme	2 mL
1 tbsp	olive oil	15 mL
8 oz	fresh tuna steak	250 g
1 tbsp	balsamic vinegar	15 mL
	Salt and freshly	
	ground pepper to taste	
	Watercress leaves	

1 In a small bowl, combine the rosemary, thyme and olive oil. Brush on both sides of the tuna.

2 Place an ungreased baking sheet under the broiler for 5 minutes, or until it is very hot.

3 Place the tuna on the hot baking sheet. Broil for 2 minutes, or until the fish is still soft to the touch but charred on the top. Do not turn the fish over.

4 Remove the fish from the oven and transfer to a platter. Pour the vinegar over the tuna and cool. Season well with salt and pepper and slice, against the grain, into slices ⅛ inch (3 mm) thick.

5 Place the tuna on individual plates, drizzle with the juices and garnish with watercress. Serve at room temperature.

Serves 4

smoked trout pâté

Combine 3 oz (90 g) boned smoked trout with 4 oz (125 g) cream cheese and 2 tbsp (25 mL) chopped onion. Add 1 tsp (5 mL) creamed horseradish and freshly ground pepper and salt to taste. Garnish with thinly sliced cucumber.

Makes about ¾ cup (175 mL)

leeks vinaigrette

This dish can be made up to three days ahead, and refrigerated until serving. Serve at room temperature.

12	leeks (dark-green leaves removed)	12

white wine vinaigrette

3 tbsp	white wine vinegar	45 mL
2 tbsp	finely chopped parsley	25 mL
1 tsp	Dijon mustard	5 mL
1	small clove garlic, minced	1
½ cup	olive or vegetable oil	125 mL
	Salt and freshly ground pepper to taste	

1	head Boston lettuce	1

1 Place the leeks in a large skillet with salted water to cover. Bring to a boil and simmer for 10 minutes. Drain well and wipe dry. (With large leeks, cut in half lengthwise through the root.) Cut off the root ends and place the leeks in a shallow dish.

2 To make the vinaigrette, beat together the vinegar, parsley, mustard and garlic in a small bowl. Slowly whisk in the oil. Season with salt and pepper. Pour the vinaigrette over the leeks and marinate at room temperature for 30 minutes.

3 Arrange Boston lettuce leaves on serving plates and place the leeks on top.

Serves 6

how to prepare leeks

Discard the dark-green outer leaves and cut off the dark-green tops, which can be frozen to use later in making stock. Split the leeks down to the root but do not separate them in half. Wash in warm running water to remove the dirt. Gently separate the leaves to make sure all the dirt is dislodged. (Warm water removes dirt more efficiently than cold.)

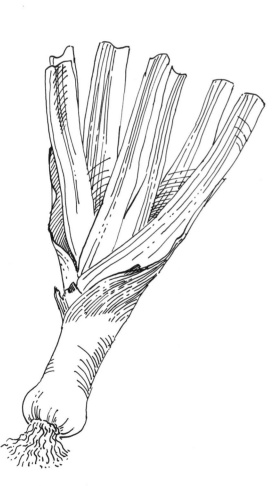

asparagus strudel

A spectacular appetizer for a special dinner. For larger crowds, the recipe can easily be doubled or tripled. Use a mild goat cheese or, if it is unavailable, use ricotta.

To turn this recipe into a substantial warm salad that can be served as a main-course lunch, arrange red and green lettuce leaves on salad plates and drizzle with Creamy Orange Vinaigrette (see page 137). Top each plate with a phyllo package cut into thirds.

12	thin stalks asparagus, cut in half	12
1 cup	slivered leeks (dark-green leaves removed)	250 mL
¼ cup	crumbled goat cheese	50 mL
1 tbsp	grated orange rind	15 mL
1 tbsp	orange juice	15 mL
½ tsp	freshly ground pepper	2 mL
1 tsp	dried tarragon	5 mL
4	sheets phyllo pastry	4
⅓ cup	butter, melted	75 mL

1 Preheat the oven to 450° F (230° C).
2 Bring a large pot of water to a boil. Add the asparagus and blanch until crisp-tender, about 1 minute. Using tongs, remove the asparagus from the pot and run under cold water until cooled.

3 Add the leeks to the pot and blanch for 1 minute. Drain and cool.

4 In a small bowl, combine the goat cheese, orange rind, orange juice, pepper and tarragon.

5 Lay 1 sheet of phyllo on a work surface. Brush with the melted butter. Place 2 tbsp (25 mL) leeks about 1 inch (2.5 cm) from the short edge of phyllo. Lay 3 half spears of asparagus on top. Spread 1 tbsp (15 mL) goat cheese mixture over the asparagus, top with 3 more spears and finish with 2 tbsp (25 mL) leeks.

6 Fold the short end of the phyllo over the mixture and brush the phyllo with butter again. Tuck in the sides of the pastry and roll up into a cylinder. Brush with butter again and place on a buttered baking sheet. Repeat with the remaining ingredients.

7 Bake for 12 minutes, or until the pastry is golden-brown. Cut each roll into thirds just before serving. Serve hot.

Serves 4

piperade

Of Basque origin, piperade is a soft scrambled egg mixture traditionally combined with onions, peppers, sausages and garlic, although you can use any meat or vegetable leftovers. Serve with toast points.

2 tbsp	olive oil	25 mL
8 oz	hot Italian sausage, sliced	250 g
1	onion, finely chopped	1
1	clove garlic, finely chopped	1
1	red pepper, finely chopped	1
10	eggs	10
2 tbsp	whipping cream	25 mL
	Salt and freshly ground pepper to taste	

1 Heat the oil in a large skillet on medium heat. Sauté the sausage until it is partially cooked, about 5 minutes.

2 Add the onion, garlic and red pepper to the skillet. Continue to sauté until the vegetables soften, about 5 minutes. Cover the skillet and cook for a further 5 minutes. Discard all but 1 tbsp (15 mL) fat.

3 In a large bowl, beat the eggs lightly just to incorporate.

4 Reduce the heat to low and add the eggs to the skillet. Stir until they are just set, about 3 minutes. Stir in the cream. Season to taste with salt and freshly ground pepper.

Serves 6

fresh spring rolls with thai dipping sauce

These fresh spring rolls are light, nutritious, low in calories and scrumptious. If rice paper wrappers are unavailable, wrap the filling ingredients in lettuce leaves. Serve these as finger food or as a first course with the sauce poured over top.

This is a very easy technique to master, and you can whip up the rolls in minutes. If fresh mint leaves are unavailable, use fresh basil, watercress, coriander or parsley.

The sweet and spicy dipping sauce is from chef Karen Barnaby. Make it as hot as you want by varying the amount of chili peppers. Unused sauce should keep in the refrigerator, covered, for up to three weeks. Fish sauce is available in Chinese grocery stores, but if you can't find it, use two chopped anchovies.

16	rice paper wrappers	16
1 oz	rice vermicelli	30 g
8	leaf lettuce leaves	8
½ cup	cooked baby shrimp	125 mL
1 cup	grated carrot	250 mL
1 cup	slivered cucumber	250 mL
2 cups	bean sprouts	500 mL
½ cup	fresh mint leaves	125 mL
8	chives or green onion leaves	8

thai dipping sauce

2 cups	granulated sugar	500 mL
1½ cups	water	375 mL
2	cloves garlic, peeled	2
½	red pepper, coarsely chopped	½
1 to 2	hot chili peppers, or Tabasco to taste	1 to 2
3 tbsp	fish sauce	45 mL
⅓ cup	lemon juice	75 mL
1 tsp	salt	5 mL
2 tbsp	grated carrot	25 mL
2 tbsp	chopped roasted peanuts	25 mL

1 Pour lukewarm water into a large bowl. Quickly immerse one rice paper wrapper at a time, making sure both sides are wet. Lay the wrappers flat on tea towels in a single layer.

2 Meanwhile, bring a large pot of water to a boil. Add the vermicelli and cook until tender, about 2 minutes. Drain and cut into 1-inch (2.5 cm) lengths.

3 Cut the lettuce leaves in half, removing the ribs. Cover each wrapper with a lettuce leaf half.

4 In a large bowl, combine the shrimp, carrot, cucumber, bean sprouts, mint and noodles.

5 Place about 1 tbsp (15 mL) shrimp mixture on the upper third of each wrapper, on top of the lettuce. Lay a chive on top of the filling. Tuck the sides in and roll up to make a neat cylinder. Continue with the remaining wrappers and filling. Cover the wrappers with a damp tea towel until needed.

6 To make the sauce, combine the sugar and water in a medium pot. Bring to a boil over high heat and cook, stirring, until the sugar has dissolved. Boil rapidly, uncovered, for 10 minutes. Remove from the heat and cool completely.

7 Place the garlic, red pepper, chili peppers and ½ cup (125 mL) sugar syrup in a food processor or blender. Blend until puréed.

8 Add the remaining syrup, fish sauce, lemon juice and salt. Blend until combined. Place the sauce in a bowl and stir in the grated carrot and peanuts. Cut the spring rolls in half and serve with the sauce.

Makes 16 rolls

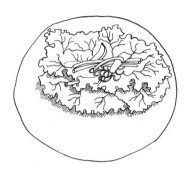

rice paper wrappers

Rice paper wrappers are used in Southeast Asian dishes to wrap cooked meats or vegetables. The translucent papers are made from rice starch and water and are dried on bamboo mats, which leave a cross-hatch of markings on the sheets.

Rice paper wrappers have to be dampened before using. There are several ways to do this, but I like to dip the wrappers in a bowl of warm water and place them on a tea towel. This way they should take about five minutes to soften.

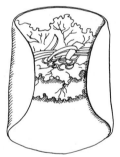

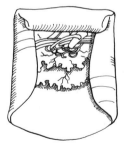

pesto-baked oysters

Pesto is a basil, pine nut and garlic paste softened with olive oil. If you don't have your own in the freezer, it can be bought in jars or tubes. Serve this as a nibbly or first course.

6	sheets phyllo pastry	6
⅓ cup	butter, melted	75 mL
¼ cup	pesto	50 mL
12	fresh or frozen shucked oysters	12

1 Preheat the oven to 375° F (190° C).
2 Lay 1 sheet of phyllo flat on the counter; brush it lightly with the butter. Lay a second sheet on top and brush again.
3 Cut the phyllo lengthwise into 4 strips.
4 Spoon the pesto on the top portion of each strip. Place an oyster on top. Fold the corner down over the filling to make a right-angled triangle. Continue as if you were folding a flag until the strip forms a neat triangle. Brush with the butter. Repeat with the remaining oysters and pastry.
5 Place the triangles on a buttered baking sheet and bake for 10 minutes, or until the pastry is golden. Serve hot.

Serves 4

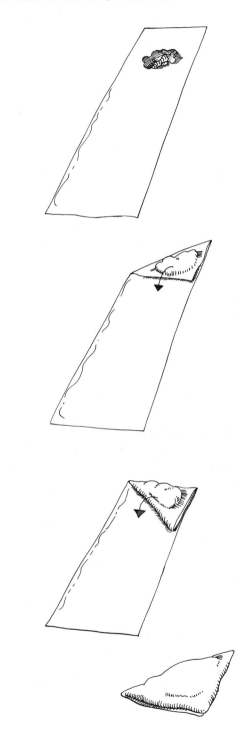

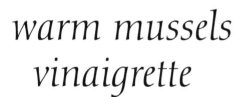

working with phyllo

Originally from the Middle East, phyllo pastry is paper-thin sheets of dough used for making flaky savouries and desserts such as baklava. Because the pastry dries out very quickly if exposed to the air, it is important to keep it covered with a damp tea towel until you are ready to work with it. Buy fresh phyllo if it is available, because the frozen product tends to tear more easily. If you can't get fresh, defrost frozen phyllo in the refrigerator overnight.

warm mussels vinaigrette

These mussels are dressed with a tangy vin-aigrette that complements their sweetness. Mop up the juices with crusty French bread.

6 lb	mussels	3 kg
¼ cup	dry white wine	50 mL
2	bay leaves	2
1 tsp	whole peppercorns	5 mL

vinaigrette

⅓ cup	red wine vinegar	75 mL
1 tsp	Dijon mustard	5 mL
⅔ cup	olive oil	150 mL
1	red onion, finely chopped	1
	freshly ground pepper to taste	
½ cup	finely chopped parsley	125 mL

1 Wash and clean the mussels, removing any hairy beards.

2 Place the white wine, bay leaves and peppercorns in a large pot. Bring to a boil on high heat. Add the mussels and cover.

3 Shake the pot a few times, uncover and remove any mussels that have popped open to a large bowl. Continue to cook, removing the mussels as they open. Discard any mussels that do not open. Heap the mussels and any juice on a large serving platter.

4 To make the vinaigrette, whisk together the vinegar and mustard in a small bowl. Slowly whisk in the oil. Stir in the onion and season with pepper. Pour over the mussels, sprinkle with the parsley and serve warm.

Serves 6 to 8

The proper way to eat mussels is with your fingers. Break off the top shell and use it to scoop out the mussel and pop it into your mouth.

omelette natasha

Making an omelette is a delicate operation, but an easy one once you know the technique. This recipe produces a sophisticated omelette with a rich smoked salmon filling.

5	eggs	5
2 tbsp	water	25 mL
	Salt and freshly	
	ground pepper to taste	
1/4 cup	finely chopped chives	50 mL
2 tbsp	butter	25 mL
1/2 cup	sour cream	125 mL
1/2 cup	chopped smoked salmon	125 mL
	(about 2 oz/60 g)	

1 In a medium bowl, with a fork, lightly combine the eggs, water, salt, pepper and 2 tbsp (25 mL) chives; don't over-beat.
2 Place a 7-inch (18 cm) omelette pan or skillet on medium-high heat. Swirl in 1 tbsp (15 mL) butter. After the butter sizzles, pour in half of the egg mixture.
3 Using a fork, swirl the centre until the mixture is firm but still moist. Tilt the pan towards you, scraping any cooked mixture at edge into the centre, then tilt the pan away from you so the uncooked mixture fills the space. Continue to do this until the entire omelette is set but still moist.

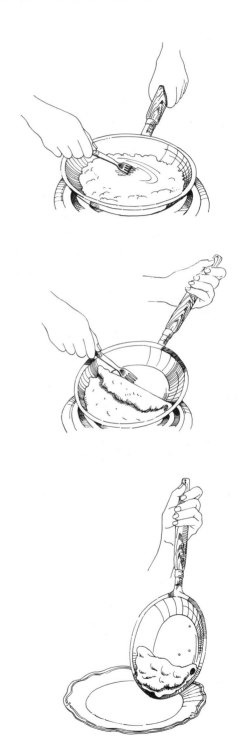

4 Spread ¼ cup (50 mL) sour cream on the top third of the omelette. Top with ¼ cup (50 mL) smoked salmon.

5 Tilt the pan, fold the top third of the omelette over and then fold over again. Slide the omelette onto a serving plate. Sprinkle with half of the remaining chives. The whole operation should take about 1 minute. Repeat for the second omelette.

Serves 2

omelette pans

To make a good omelette, it is important to have a good omelette pan. They are usually about 7 inches (18 cm) in diameter and are made of a heavy material such as aluminum, cast iron or cast-iron enamel. Omelette pans should be seasoned to prevent sticking, and they should be used exclusively for making omelettes and crêpes.

To season the pan, fill it halfway with vegetable oil. On high heat, heat the oil until it is smoking. Carefully remove the pan from the heat and let it sit for 24 hours. Pour the oil off and wipe out the pan. Omelette pans should not be washed. After they have been used, wipe them out with salt (which acts as an abrasive) and rub them with a little oil.

The fresher eggs are, the better they taste. There is no difference in taste between brown and white eggs. To determine whether an egg is fresh, place it in a pot of water. Old, stale eggs will rise to the surface, while fresh ones will stay submerged.

omelettes

Omelettes can be whipped up any time of the day or night to fill a hunger pang or feed a friend who has dropped by unexpectedly. Grated cheese, crumbled bacon, sautéed mushrooms or leftover chicken or fish can be folded into the omelette centre. Never overcook an omelette; it should always be moist in the centre.

23

brie and cheddar pudding

This easy brunch recipe is a real hit in my cooking classes. You can add chopped cooked vegetables or bacon for a more quiche-like dish. The pudding has a real cheesy, custard consistency, and no one will know there is bread in it. Serve it with Fruit Salsa or Sweet and Sour Peaches. Combine the bread and cheeses ahead of time and pour the egg/milk mixture over up to two hours before baking.

8 to 10	slices white bread, crusts removed	8 to 10
⅓ cup	butter, melted	75 mL
8 oz	Brie cheese, rind removed, cut into cubes	250 g
1 cup	grated old Cheddar cheese (about 4 oz/125 g)	250 mL
4	eggs	4
1½ cups	milk	375 mL
1 tbsp	Dijon mustard	15 mL
2 tbsp	finely chopped green onion	25 mL
pinch	salt	pinch
pinch	freshly ground pepper	pinch
pinch	cayenne pepper	pinch
pinch	paprika	pinch

1 Line a deep 11 x 7-inch (2 L) buttered baking dish with half the bread slices. Brush with half the melted butter.
2 Top the bread with half the Brie and half the Cheddar. Repeat with the remaining bread, butter and cheeses.
3 In a large bowl, mix the eggs with the milk, mustard, green onion, salt, pepper and cayenne. Pour over the bread. Let stand for 30 minutes. Sprinkle with the paprika.
4 Preheat the oven to 375° F (190° C).
5 Bake the pudding for 30 to 40 minutes, or until puffed and brown. Allow to cool slightly before serving.
Serves 6

fruit salsa

In a serving bowl, combine 2 chopped apples, 2 chopped pears, 1 diced pineapple and 1 diced honeydew melon. (You can also stir in ½ cup/125 mL chopped dried apricots and ½ cup/125 mL chopped almonds.) The salsa should keep for up to three days in the refrigerator. Use any leftovers as a topping for ice cream, cereal, French toast or pancakes.
Makes about 6 cups (1.5 L)

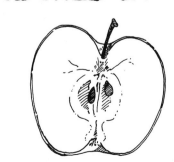

sweet and sour peaches

Slice 4 fresh peaches and place in a bowl. In a pot, combine ⅓ cup (75 mL) cider vinegar, ⅓ cup (75 mL) peach jam and ½ tsp (2 mL) ground cumin. Bring to a boil and pour over the peaches. Cool before serving. This should keep, refrigerated, for two weeks.

Makes 3 cups (750 mL)

do-it-yourself tostadas

A good project for the whole family. Change the toppings with your family's taste in mind.

4	flour tortillas	4
2 cups	grated Cheddar cheese	500 mL

toppings

½ cup	salsa, homemade or store bought	125 mL
4 cups	shredded iceberg lettuce	1 L
½ cup	sour cream	125 mL
3	green onions, chopped	3

1 Preheat oven to 400 F (200 C). Lightly oil a baking sheet.
2 Sprinkle tortillas with cheese. Place on baking sheet and bake 3 to 4 minutes, or until cheese melts.
3 Place salsa, lettuce, sour cream and green onions in separate bowls.
4 Serve warm tortillas beside bowls of toppings. Fold tortilla over toppings for easy eating.
Serves 4

oat bran pancakes

Oat bran is high in fibre and makes a healthy pancake for breakfast or brunch. Serve with Blueberry Sauce or maple syrup. You can also fold fresh blueberries or a mashed banana into the pancake batter.

½ cup	all-purpose flour	125 mL
½ cup	oat bran	125 mL
1 tsp	baking soda	5 mL
pinch	salt	pinch
2 tsp	granulated sugar	10 mL
1	egg	1
1	egg white	1
¾ cup	buttermilk	175 mL
1 tbsp	butter, melted, or vegetable oil	15 mL

1 In a medium bowl, combine the flour, oat bran, baking soda, salt and sugar.
2 In a separate bowl, mix together the egg, egg white and buttermilk.
3 Add the wet ingredients to the dry ingredients and combine. Mix in the butter.
4 Heat a large skillet or griddle on medium heat and brush with oil. Ladle a heaping 2 tbsp (25 mL) batter onto the griddle, spreading it into a 3-inch (7.5 cm) circle. Cook until bubbles appear on the surface, about 1 minute. Flip over and brown on the other side. Continue until all the batter is used. Serve with Blueberry Sauce.

Makes about 12 pancakes

blueberry sauce

In a medium pot, combine 2 cups (500 mL) frozen or fresh blueberries with the juice of 1 lemon and 1 tbsp (15 mL) granulated sugar. Heat until the sugar dissolves. Scrape half of the mixture into a food processor or blender and purée. Return the purée to the pot and combine with the remaining blueberries. Serve warm.

Makes about 2 cups (500 mL)

bruschetta

Bruschetta, pronounced "brusketta," traditionally is toasted bread rubbed with garlic and brushed with olive oil. Today in many restaurants it comes topped with tomatoes, basil and sometimes garlic and cheese. Try our traditional version as well as the tomato-topped variation. Serve as an hors d'oeuvre or as a salad accompaniment.

1 loaf	Italian bread	1
1/4 cup	olive oil	50 mL
1	clove garlic, cut in half	1

1 Slice bread on the diagonal into 1/2-inch (1.25 cm) thick slices. Grill or toast until golden on each side, about 1 minute. Brush with olive oil and rub with garlic.

tomato topping

3	tomatoes, chopped	3
2 tbsp	finely chopped fresh basil	25 mL
1	clove garlic, crushed	1
2 tbsp	olive oil	25 mL
1/4 cup	grated Parmesan cheese	50 mL
	Salt and freshly ground pepper to taste	

1 Combine all ingredients. Pile on top of garlic rubbed toasts.
Serves 6

salad pizza

A thin pizza dough that ensures a crisp crust. Ready-to-bake pizza dough is available at supermarkets and bakeries, and you can even use already baked pizza base. Just sprinkle on goat cheese and garlic and bake for 10 minutes at 350 F (180 C) to reheat. It will not have the crispness that an unbaked dough will have. You can prebake the pizza and reheat just before serving.

pizza dough

1 tsp	granulated sugar	5 mL
1 cup	warm water	250 mL
1 1/2 tsp	dry active yeast	7 mL
3 cups	all-purpose flour	750 mL
1 tsp	salt	5 mL
1/4 cup	olive oil	50 mL
	Cornmeal	

topping

1 tbsp	olive oil	15 mL
2	cloves garlic, sliced	2
1 cup	crumbled goat cheese	250 mL
1/4 cup	grated Parmesan cheese	50 mL
1 tbsp	chopped fresh basil	15 mL

salad

2 tbsp	balsamic vinegar	25 mL
1 tsp	Dijon mustard	5 mL
2 tbsp	olive oil	25 mL
	Salt and freshly ground pepper to taste	
6 cups	mixed lettuce or mesclun	1.5 L
1/4 cup	chopped chives	50 mL

1 Dissolve sugar in warm water. Sprinkle over yeast and let stand until dissolved. Leave for 5 minutes, or until yeast mixture bubbles.

2 In a food processor or an electric mixer with a dough hook, add flour and salt. With machine running, pour in yeast mixture and oil and process until dough forms. If dough seems slightly sticky, beat in another 1/4 cup (50 mL) flour.

3 Remove dough from processor and place in oiled bowl. Turn dough in bowl until coated with oil. Cover with tea towel and place in warm place until doubled in bulk, about 1 1/2 hours with regular yeast, 45 minutes with fast-rising yeast.

4 Punch dough down and divide into 2 balls. Reserve one ball for another use. Either freeze for up to 6 months or cover tightly and refrigerate for up to 5 days.

5 Preheat oven to 500 F (250 C) for 20 minutes.

6 Place second ball on lightly floured surface. Flour dough lightly and roll out into 12-inch (30 cm) round, leaving edges slightly thicker.

7 Place dough on cornmeal-dusted pizza pan or pizza stone on lower rack of oven. Top with oil, garlic, goat cheese, Parmesan and basil. Bake about 8 to 10 minutes, or until crust is golden.

8 To make salad dressing, whisk vinegar and mustard together. Whisk in olive oil and season with salt and pepper. Reserve salad dressing.

9 Toss salad vegetables together in a large bowl and drizzle with vinaigrette. As soon as pizza comes out of oven, top with salad. Cut into four slices at the table.

Serves 4

28

chapter three

SOUPS

M*any people think of homemade soups as concoctions that need to simmer on the stove for several hours – hardly ideal for the fast cook. But the soups in this chapter are simple and quick to prepare. One of soup's great attributes is that it usually needs little attention while it is cooking, giving you time to do other things.*

Many of these are light, first-course soups suitable for entertaining, or a great way to stretch a family meal; a few are heartier main-dish soups, which are perfect for a light dinner or lunch when accompanied by biscuits or bread and a salad.

tips

- Good soup requires good stock. Although homemade stock may seem like too much trouble, there are shortcuts besides using salty and MSG-laden bouillon cubes. Try canned chicken or beef broth diluted with equal parts of water (the low-salt broths are the best). Or make the quick stock recipes in this chapter – they are worth the modest amount of time it takes to put them together.

- Soup can be turned into elegant fare with the addition of a simple garnish. Try sprinkling soup with chopped parsley or other fresh herbs. Garnish a cream soup with grated, chopped or fried pieces of the main ingredient. Sprinkle on herb-, garlic- or cheese-flavoured croutons. Or try streaking cream, sour cream or pesto over the surface of the soup in swirls or designs.

- Seemingly ordinary ingredients can be turned into all sorts of inventive soups. For the simplest soup, simmer a few leftover cooked or raw vegetables and/or leftover salad with some cooked meat or fish and some stock or water. Season with spices and herbs. Call it "cleaning-out-the-refrigerator soup"!

quick chicken stock

In place of chicken pieces, you can use the bones from a leftover roast chicken. Keep this stock on hand for sauces, soups and other dishes that require chicken stock. It can be refrigerated for up to five days, or you can freeze it.

8 oz	chicken legs or breasts	250 g
½	bay leaf	½
pinch	dried thyme	pinch
1	small onion, chopped	1
¼ cup	chopped celery	50 mL
½ cup	chopped carrot	125 mL
3	mushrooms, chopped	3
3	stalks parsley	3
3	whole peppercorns	3

1 Place all the ingredients in a large pot. Cover with 6 cups (1.5 L) water.

2 Bring to a boil on high heat; skim off the scum. Reduce the heat to low and simmer, uncovered, for 25 minutes. Strain.

Makes 4 cups (1 L) stock

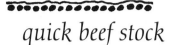

quick beef stock

Quick beef stock can be made by the same method as Quick Chicken Stock, but substitute 8 oz (250 g) lean hamburger for the chicken.

quick fish stock

In a medium pot, combine 1 cup (250 mL) clam juice, 3 cups (750 mL) water, 1 sliced onion, 1 sliced carrot, 1 bay leaf and 1 stalk parsley. Bring to a boil on high heat, reduce the heat to low and simmer for 20 minutes. Strain and cool before using. Refrigerate for up to one week or freeze until needed.

Makes 4 cups (1 L)

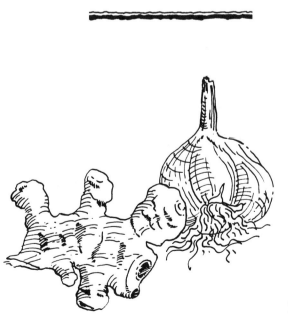

mushroom and mustard soup

A favourite soup that is easy to make. The mushrooms themselves act as the thickener and the mustard brings out a rich mushroom flavour.

2 tbsp	butter	25 mL
1 cup	chopped red onion	250 mL
12 oz	mushrooms, sliced	375 g
2 tbsp	dry sherry	25 mL
1 tbsp	Dijon mustard	15 mL
2 cups	chicken stock	500 mL
½ cup	whipping cream	125 mL
	Salt and freshly ground pepper to taste	
2 tbsp	chopped chives	25 mL

1 Heat the butter in a medium pot on medium heat until sizzling. Add the onion and mushrooms. Sauté for about 2 minutes, or until the mushrooms are softened.
2 Stir in the sherry, mustard and stock. Bring to a boil, turn the heat to low, cover and simmer for 5 minutes.
3 In a blender or food processor, purée the soup until the mushrooms are chopped but not completely smooth. Return to the pot, add the cream and simmer for 5 minutes. Season with salt and pepper and garnish with the chives before serving.

Serves 3 to 4

cream of sweet potato soup

Underrated sweet potatoes have suffered from a surfeit of sugar in their cooking; try this rich complex-tasting soup made without any added sweetness. Garnish with sage croutons before serving.

2 tbsp	butter	25 mL
1 tbsp	chopped fresh ginger	15 mL
2	small leeks	2
	(dark-green leaves removed)	
2	large sweet potatoes,	2
	peeled and diced	
1 tsp	ground cumin	5 mL
¼ tsp	grated nutmeg	1 mL
1 tsp	ground coriander	5 mL
pinch	cayenne pepper	pinch
3 cups	chicken stock	750 mL
¼ cup	whipping cream	50 mL
	Salt and freshly	
	ground pepper to taste	
2 tbsp	lime juice	25 mL

1 Melt the butter in a medium pot on medium heat. Add the ginger, leeks and sweet potatoes. Sauté until the vegetables are softened slightly, about 2 minutes. Sprinkle in the cumin, nutmeg, coriander and cayenne. Stir together.

2 Pour in the chicken stock and bring to a boil. Lower the heat, cover and simmer for 15 minutes, or until the sweet potatoes are tender.

3 Purée the soup in a food processor or blender until smooth. Return to the pot, add the cream, bring to a boil, reduce heat and simmer for 5 minutes. Season well with salt, pepper and lime juice.

Serves 4

sage croutons

You can also flavour these croutons with garlic or other herbs. Sprinkle the croutons on top of soup just before serving.

Cut 2 slices of bread into cubes. Heat 2 tbsp (25 mL) olive oil in a large skillet on high heat. Add the bread and 2 tbsp (25 mL) chopped fresh sage (or 2 tsp/ 10 mL dried). Toss together until the bread is golden-brown. Drain on paper towels.

Makes about 1 cup (250 mL)

soup enhancers

If a soup tastes bland, goose it up with lemon or lime juice, salt, pepper, fresh or dried herbs, minced garlic or a spoonful of tomato paste.

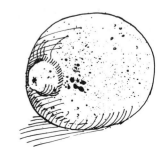

red, green and yellow pepperpot soup

Sweet peppers make a wonderfully rich soup, and when you use the three colours, the end result is a beautiful orange. However, use whatever peppers you can find. If you have a few that are past their best, this recipe is a good way to use them up.

1	red pepper	1
1	green pepper	1
1	yellow pepper	1
1 tbsp	butter	15 mL
1	leek (dark-green leaves removed), sliced	1
1 tbsp	finely chopped fresh ginger	15 mL
1 tsp	curry powder	5 mL
4 cups	chicken stock	1 L
¼ cup	whipping cream	50 mL
	Salt and freshly ground pepper to taste	
pinch	granulated sugar	pinch

1 Core and seed the peppers and chop them coarsely. Finely chop ¼ cup (50 mL) of each colour and reserve.

2 In a medium pot on medium-high heat, melt the butter. Add the leek, ginger and peppers. Lower the heat to medium, cover and simmer for 10 minutes.

3 Stir in the curry powder and continue to cook for 1 minute. Pour in the stock, bring to a boil and simmer, uncovered, for 10 minutes, or until the peppers are soft.

4 In a food processor or blender, purée the soup until smooth. Return the soup to the pot. Add the cream and simmer for 5 minutes, adjusting the seasonings by adding salt, pepper and sugar.

5 Just before serving, garnish each bowl of soup with a sprinkle of finely chopped peppers.

Serves 4 to 6

spinach soup with shrimp

The pink shrimp contrast with the dark-green colour of the soup. If there is any soup left over, it will taste great cold with a dollop of sour cream.

2 tbsp	butter	25 mL
½ cup	chopped onion	125 mL
1 tbsp	all-purpose flour	15 mL
3 cups	chicken stock	750 mL
10 oz	fresh spinach, washed	300 g
1 tbsp	finely chopped fresh dill, or 1 tsp (5 mL) dried	15 mL
	Salt and freshly ground pepper to taste	
¼ cup	whipping cream	50 mL
1 tsp	lemon juice	5 mL
½ cup	cooked baby shrimp, chilled	125 mL

1 Heat the butter in a medium pot on medium heat until sizzling. Add the onion and sauté until softened, about 2 minutes.
2 Stir in the flour. Cook for 1 minute, stirring, then add the stock, spinach and dill. Continue stirring, bring to a boil. Reduce the heat and simmer, uncovered, for 10 minutes. Season with salt and pepper.
3 Purée the soup in a food processor or blender until the spinach is finely chopped.
4 Return the soup to the pot, add the cream and simmer for 2 minutes, or until the tastes are combined. Stir in the lemon juice. Garnish with the chilled shrimp before serving.
Serves 4

cold cucumber soup

This soup has a crispness similar to raita, the customary coolant that accompanies many spicy East Indian dishes.

1 cup	grated cucumber, plus 4 thin slices	250 mL
1 cup	plain yogourt	250 mL
½ cup	chicken stock	125 mL
½ cup	tomato juice	125 mL
1 tbsp	grated fresh ginger	15 mL
1	clove garlic, minced	1
2 tbsp	tarragon vinegar	25 mL
2 tbsp	light cream	25 mL
2 tbsp	finely chopped fresh mint	25 mL
	Salt and freshly ground pepper to taste	

1 In a medium bowl, blend together the grated cucumber, yogourt, stock and tomato juice. Add the ginger, garlic, vinegar, cream and 1 tbsp (15 mL) mint. Season with salt and pepper and chill.
2 Serve cold with a garnish of cucumber slices and the remaining mint.
Serves 4

watercress and lemon soup

This soup may be served either hot or cold.

2 tbsp	butter	25 mL
1	onion, chopped	1
2	potatoes, peeled and diced	2
3 cups	chicken stock	750 mL
1 tbsp	lemon juice	15 mL
1	bunch watercress	1
⅓ cup	whipping cream	75 mL
	Salt and freshly ground pepper to taste	
1 tbsp	grated lemon rind	15 mL

1 Heat the butter in a large pot on medium heat. Add the onion and potatoes and sauté until coated with the butter, about 2 minutes.

2 Add the chicken stock and lemon juice. Bring to a boil, then simmer, uncovered, for 5 minutes.

3 Meanwhile, divide the bunch of watercress into two. Chop one half and add both the leaves and the stems to the soup. Cook until the potatoes are tender, 10 to 15 minutes longer.

4 Strip the leaves from the second bunch of watercress and discard the stalks.

5 Purée the soup in a food processor or blender until smooth. Return the soup to the pot and add the cream. Simmer for 5 minutes to combine the flavours, stir in the watercress leaves and simmer another minute. Season with salt and pepper. Garnish each serving with the grated lemon rind before serving.

Serves 4

watercress

Store watercress head down in a bowl of water in the refrigerator. Because watercress breathes through its leaves, it should stay fresh for up to one week. Watercress also makes a pretty garnish. Gather a small bunch in your hand, break off the stalks and lay the leaves on a plate.

serving suggestions for cold soups

- Chill glass mugs or wine glasses. Wet the rims and dip them in finely chopped herbs such as parsley or dill. Pour in the soup and refrigerate.
- Serve cold soups in bowls and swirl whipping cream across the surface.
- Freeze scooped-out halves of papaya, oranges, grapefruit or cantaloupe. Fill the frozen fruit with cold soups. Serve at once.

fresh mint and spinach soup

A soup with a refreshing Thai flavour to make for special guests in the summer when your garden is overrun with mint. The soup can be served hot or cold and is great before a barbecue.

1 tbsp	vegetable oil	15 mL
4	shallots or green onions, finely chopped	4
2 tbsp	finely chopped fresh ginger	25 mL
1 tsp	chopped green chili	5 mL
4 cups	chicken stock	1 L
½ cup	canned coconut milk	125 mL
4 cups	shredded fresh spinach	1 L
¼ cup	chopped fresh mint	50 mL
1 tbsp	lime juice	15 mL
	Salt and freshly ground pepper to taste	

1 In a medium pot, heat the oil on medium heat. Add the shallots, ginger and chili. Sauté until softened, about 3 minutes.
2 Pour in the chicken stock and coconut milk. Bring to a boil and simmer, uncovered, for 5 minutes. Add the spinach, mint and lime juice. Cook for another 10 minutes, or until the spinach is wilted. Season with salt and pepper.
Serves 4

carrot zucchini soup

For a complete meal, serve this soup with some crusty bread and a few slices of cheese.

1 tbsp	butter	15 mL
½ cup	chopped onion	125 mL
2	carrots, chopped	2
2	potatoes, peeled and diced	2
2	medium zucchini, chopped	2
½ tsp	ground cumin	2 mL
1	bay leaf	1
2 cups	chicken stock	500 mL
1 cup	milk	250 mL
	Salt and freshly ground pepper to taste	

1 In a medium pot on medium heat, melt the butter. Add the onion, carrots, potatoes and zucchini. Cook, covered, for 5 minutes.
2 Stir in the cumin, bay leaf, stock and milk. Bring to a boil, then simmer, uncovered, for 15 to 20 minutes, or until the vegetables are tender. Remove the bay leaf.
3 Purée the soup in a food processor or blender until smooth. Return to the pot, season with salt and pepper and simmer for 5 minutes to combine the flavours.
Serves 3 to 4

salmon chowder

This thick, hearty soup can be made with leftover cooked or canned salmon. For a special treat, add 2 oz (60 mL) chopped smoked salmon just before serving.

2 tbsp	butter	25 mL
1	small onion, chopped	1
2 tbsp	all-purpose flour	25 mL
3 cups	milk	750 mL
2	potatoes, peeled and diced	2
2 cups	cooked fresh salmon, flaked, or 2 6½-oz (184 g) cans	500 mL
1 tbsp	lemon juice	15 mL
	Salt and freshly ground pepper to taste	
2 tbsp	finely chopped fresh dill, or 2 tsp (10 mL) dried	25 mL

1 Melt the butter in a medium pot on medium heat. Add the onion and sauté until softened, about 3 minutes. Stir in the flour and cook, stirring, for another minute.
2 Pour in the milk and bring to a boil, stirring. Add the potatoes and cook, covered, until the potatoes are softened, about 10 minutes.
3 Stir in the salmon and simmer for another 5 minutes. Season with the lemon juice, salt, pepper and dill.
Serves 4

fennel almond soup

Save some of the feathery tops of the fennel for garnishing the soup. When it is cooked, fennel loses most of its licorice-like taste and becomes mellow and delicate.

2 tbsp	butter	25 mL
1	onion, sliced	1
2	bulbs fennel, sliced	2
¼ cup	ground almonds	50 mL
4 cups	chicken stock	1 L
½ cup	whipping cream	125 mL
	Salt and freshly ground pepper to taste	
¼ cup	slivered almonds, toasted	50 mL

1 In a large pot, melt the butter on medium heat. Add the onion and fennel and sauté until slightly softened, about 3 minutes.
2 Add the ground almonds and chicken stock and bring to a boil. Lower the heat and simmer, uncovered, for 20 minutes, or until the vegetables are soft.
3 Purée the soup in a food processor or blender until smooth. Return to the pot and add the cream. Bring to a boil and simmer for 5 minutes. Season well with salt and pepper. Garnish with fennel sprigs and slivered almonds before serving.
Serves 6

jamaican squash soup

A thick spicy soup but with surprisingly few calories – only about 100 per serving, if you use low-fat yogourt.

1 tbsp	vegetable oil	15 mL
3	leeks (dark-green leaves removed), thinly sliced	3
1	carrot, thinly sliced	1
1	medium butternut squash, peeled and diced	1
½ tsp	ground allspice	2 mL
½ tsp	ground cinnamon	2 mL
1 tsp	dried thyme	5 mL
½ tsp	dried chili flakes	2 mL
6 cups	chicken stock	1.5 L
½ cup	whipping cream or low-fat plain yogourt	125 mL
	Salt to taste	
2 tbsp	chopped chives	25 mL

1 Heat the oil in a large pot on medium-high heat. Add the leeks, carrot and squash and sauté until softened, about 3 minutes. Add the allspice, cinnamon, thyme and chili flakes.

2 Stir in the stock, bring to a boil, reduce the heat and simmer, uncovered, for 20 minutes, or until the vegetables are tender. Purée the soup in a food processor or blender until smooth.

3 Return the soup to the pot. Add the cream and bring to a boil. Simmer for 5 minutes. Taste for seasoning, adding salt as required. Garnish with the chopped chives before serving.

Serves 6

allspice

Allspice is the pimento berry; it is picked almost ripe and then sun-dried. Its flavour is similar to a pungent mixture of cinnamon, nutmeg and cloves. Most allspice comes from Jamaica. You can buy it whole or ground, but the whole berries stay fresh longer. Grind them in a pepper mill when needed. Use nutmeg if allspice is not available.

If you use yogourt, sour cream or light cream instead of whipping cream in a soup, do not bring the soup to a boil because they will separate. Reheat the soup slowly until it is simmering, then serve.

If your soup is too salty, cut a large potato into quarters and add it to the soup. Cook the soup until the potato is soft, then remove it. The potato will soak up some of the salt.

cabbage, bacon and potato soup

Stick-to-your-ribs soup, very warm and comforting. If you have leftover cooked sausage, use it instead of the bacon.

2 lb	**potatoes, peeled (about 6 medium)**	**1 kg**
12 oz	**bacon, diced**	**375 mL**
1	**clove garlic, finely chopped**	**1**
3 cups	**finely shredded cabbage**	**750 mL**
2 tbsp	**cider vinegar**	**25 mL**
¼ cup	**whipping cream**	**50 mL**
	Salt and freshly	
	ground pepper to taste	
¼ cup	**chopped chives or**	**50 mL**
	green onion tops	

1 In a large pot, cover the potatoes with 5 cups (1.25 L) water. Cover, bring to a boil and simmer for 15 minutes, or until tender.

2 With a fork or potato masher, break up the potatoes. (Do not drain.) They should be lumpy, not smooth.

3 Meanwhile, in a large skillet on medium heat, cook the bacon until crisp. Remove the bacon and drain off all but 2 tbsp (25 mL) fat.

4 Add the garlic and cabbage to the skillet and sauté until the cabbage is wilted, about 3 minutes. Sprinkle on the vinegar and add the cream. Simmer on low heat until the cabbage is crisp-tender, about 10 minutes.

5 Add the cabbage, its liquid and the diced bacon to the potatoes and water in the pot. Simmer everything together until the tastes are combined, about 5 minutes. Season well with salt and pepper. Sprinkle with the chives before serving.

Serves 6

parsnip chowder

Chowder comes from the French word chaudière – a large cauldron that sailors used to make fish stews. Today it refers to any kind of chunky soup. Substitute carrots or turnips for the parsnips, if desired.

4 oz	peameal bacon, diced	125 g
1	large red onion, chopped	1
2	potatoes, peeled and diced	2
4	parsnips, peeled and diced	4
3 cups	chicken stock	750 mL
1 tsp	dried thyme	5 mL
pinch	cayenne pepper	pinch
2 cups	light cream or milk	500 mL
¼ cup	finely chopped parsley	50 mL
1 tsp	paprika	5 mL

1 In a large pot on medium heat, cook the bacon until it renders its fat. Add the onion and sauté for 2 to 3 minutes, or until soft.
2 Add the potatoes and parsnips to the pot and continue to sauté until they are coated in the bacon fat.
3 Pour in the stock and add the thyme and cayenne. Bring to a boil, lower the heat and simmer, covered, for 20 minutes, or until the vegetables are tender.
4 Add the cream and parsley. Simmer gently for 5 minutes. Garnish with a sprinkling of paprika before serving.
Serves 6

parsnips

Parsnips are an underrated vegetable with a rich, sweet taste. They make an especially rich, creamy-coloured cake (substitute parsnips for carrots in any carrot cake recipe), and when mixed with carrots or potatoes, they make superb gratins. Try to buy medium-sized, cream-coloured parsnips. The large ones often have woody centres and the darker brown ones are past their prime.

quick winter vegetable soup

Most vegetable soups are cooked for hours, but this light, fresh version simmers only long enough to leave the vegetables just tender. To make this soup more substantial, add 8 oz (250 g) sliced, sautéed Polish sausage with the pasta.

2 tbsp	olive oil	25 mL
1	onion, diced	1
1	leek (dark-green leaves removed), thickly sliced	1
1 cup	diced turnip	250 mL
1 cup	diced potato	250 mL
1 cup	diced carrot	250 mL

1	clove garlic, finely chopped	1
5 cups	chicken stock	1.25 L
½ cup	macaroni	125 mL
1 cup	shredded fresh spinach	250 mL
	Salt and freshly	
	ground pepper to taste	
¼ cup	grated Parmesan cheese	50 mL

1 Heat the olive oil in a large pot on medium heat. Add the onion and leek and sauté until coated with the oil, about 2 minutes.

2 Add the turnip, potato, carrot and garlic and continue to cook, stirring, for about 3 minutes.

3 Add the stock and bring to a boil. Reduce the heat and simmer for 10 minutes. Add the pasta and simmer for 10 minutes longer, or until the vegetables are crisp-tender and the pasta is cooked.

4 Add the spinach and cook for 5 minutes longer, or until the spinach is wilted. Season with salt and pepper. Sprinkle with the Parmesan before serving.

Serves 6

orzo

Orzo is a rice- or barley-shaped pasta that is used in soups or cooked and sautéed in herbed butter as a side dish. It can be found in many supermarkets and Italian grocery stores.

sicilian onion soup

A rich onion and tomato soup to serve before a simple main course.

2 tbsp	olive oil	25 mL
2	Spanish onions, thinly sliced	2
pinch	granulated sugar	pinch
2	cloves garlic, finely chopped	2
1 tsp	dried basil	5 mL
½ tsp	dried oregano	2 mL
1	bay leaf	1
2 cups	chopped tomatoes	500 mL
3 cups	chicken stock	750 mL
½ cup	orzo	125 mL
	Salt and freshly	
	ground pepper to taste	
3 tbsp	finely chopped parsley	45 mL
¼ cup	grated Parmesan cheese	50 mL

1 In a large pot, heat the oil on medium heat. Add the onions, sugar, garlic, basil and oregano. Sauté until the onions turn light-brown, about 10 minutes.

2 Add the bay leaf, tomatoes and chicken stock. Bring to a boil and simmer for 10 minutes.

3 Add the pasta and simmer, uncovered, until the pasta is tender, about 10 minutes more. Season with salt and pepper. Stir in the parsley. Sprinkle the soup with Parmesan cheese just before serving.

Serves 6

leafy greens soup

This fresh and elegant soup is delicately tangy in flavour and is superb as the starter for a special dinner. Serve it before Peppered Beef with Peppery Sauce (see page 84). If sorrel is unavailable, use spinach. The soup can also be served cold.

3 tbsp	butter	45 mL
2	bunches green onions, chopped	2
2 tbsp	all-purpose flour	25 mL
1	head Boston lettuce, shredded	1
2 cups	shredded sorrel leaves	500 mL
1 cup	fresh or frozen peas	250 mL
pinch	granulated sugar	pinch
4 cups	chicken stock	1 L
½ cup	whipping cream	125 mL
	Salt and freshly ground pepper to taste	
2 tbsp	finely chopped fresh mint or parsley	25 mL

1 In a large pot, heat the butter on medium heat until sizzling. Add the green onions and sauté for 3 minutes, or until they soften. Stir in the flour and cook, stirring constantly, for 2 minutes.
2 Stir in the lettuce, sorrel, peas and sugar. Add the chicken stock and bring to a boil, stirring. Reduce the heat, cover and simmer for 20 minutes, or until the vegetables are tender.

3 Purée the soup in a food processor or blender until smooth. Return to the pot, add the cream and simmer for 5 minutes. Season with salt and pepper and sprinkle with fresh mint before serving.
Serves 6 to 8

sorrel

Sorrel is a relative of rhubarb and has a lemony, tart flavour. It looks similar to spinach and is often available in the spring and summer. It can be used in soups or to make sauces for fish. Sorrel has a short refrigerator life and should be used within two days of purchase.

chapter four

FISH & SHELLFISH

Traditionally, fish and shellfish have not been a big part of the Canadian diet. But all this is changing because seafood has lots of benefits, and it's perfect for the person in a hurry. As Canadian consumption goes up and demand increases, more and more varieties of fish are coming on the market.

Fish and shellfish are simple to prepare, cook quickly and are very versatile. They are also high in protein and low in fat, and fish is exceptionally low in cholesterol. There is even evidence that fish oil may help prevent heart attacks.

tips

- Look for whole fish that has a clear eye. Cloudiness or a sunken eye means the fish isn't fresh.
- If you press fish with your finger, the flesh should spring right back. If it feels spongy, don't buy it.
- Fish and shellfish should always smell fresh and not have a "fishy" odour.
- When you are buying whole fish, look under the gills; they should be bright red. If the gills are pink or brownish, the fish has been out of the water too long.
- Fish fillets should look translucent and feel firm to the touch. If buying fish steaks, select centre-cut steaks; they are usually more tender than the ones from the tail.
- Knowing a good fish market is one of the best ways to make sure you are getting good seafood. You should be able to trust your fishmonger to tell you how fresh the seafood is, or whether it has been frozen and thawed. (Most shrimp, for example, is frozen on the ships when caught.)
- If you buy frozen fish (some firmer-fleshed varieties freeze well), always defrost it in the refrigerator overnight to reduce the loss of natural moisture.
- Try not to keep fresh seafood for longer than one day; it spoils quickly. Remove it from any plastic wrap and place it in a dish. Cover with a paper towel and store it in the coldest part of your refrigerator. If you cannot use fish within a day, rub it with soy sauce or yogourt to help it last a bit longer.

poached salmon fillets

Poaching fish is a necessary technique for every cook to learn. If you want to poach a whole fish, do not remove bones because they keep the fish moist. For cold poached salmon, place fish in a fish poacher in cold water combined with wine, lemon slices and seasonings. Liquid should come halfway up the fish. Bring to a boil covered, simmer 2 minutes, then remove from heat and let cool in stock. The fish will be perfectly cooked.

1 cup	white wine	250 mL
1 cup	fish or chicken stock	250 mL
1	bay leaf	1
1 tsp each	dried thyme, peppercorns	5 mL
6	6-oz (180 gm) salmon fillets	6
1/4 cup	unsalted butter or whipping cream	50 mL
1/4 cup	chopped fresh coriander, parsley or dill	50 mL

1 In a large skillet, bring to a boil white wine, stock, bay leaf, thyme and peppercorns.
2 Plunge in salmon fillets, and simmer gently, covered, for 3 to 5 minutes, or until white juices just begin to rise up. Remove salmon from liquid.
3 Bring liquid to a boil in skillet and reduce. Whisk in butter or cream. Serve over salmon and garnish with coriander.
Serves 6

salmon asparagus stir-fry

When you are in the mood for a Chinese dish, try this delightful blend of flavours, textures and colours. Serve it on a platter surrounded by puffed rice noodles. The noodles can be prepared in advance and served cold.

1	**1-lb (500 g) salmon fillet**	1
2 tbsp	**dry white wine**	25 mL
1 tsp	**granulated sugar**	5 mL
2 tbsp	**soy sauce**	25 mL
8 oz	**thin asparagus stalks**	250 g
½ cup	**chicken stock**	125 mL
2 tsp	**white or rice vinegar**	10 mL
1 tbsp	**oyster sauce**	15 mL
1 tsp	**sesame oil**	5 mL
2 tbsp	**vegetable oil**	25 mL
1	**slice ginger, smashed**	1
2 tsp	**cornstarch mixed with**	10 mL
	1 tbsp (15 mL) water	
1	**green onion, finely chopped**	1

1 Skin the salmon and slice crosswise into ¼-inch (5 mm) slices.

2 In a large bowl, combine the wine, sugar and soy sauce. Add the salmon and marinate for 30 minutes.

3 Slice the asparagus into 2-inch (5 cm) lengths and set aside.

4 In a small bowl or measuring cup, combine the chicken stock, vinegar, oyster sauce and sesame oil; reserve.

5 Heat the vegetable oil in a wok or large skillet on high heat until very hot. Add the salmon slices and stir-fry for 30 seconds, or until they turn pink. Remove from the wok.

6 Add the ginger and the asparagus and stir-fry for 1 minute. Pour in the reserved chicken stock mixture. Bring to a boil and add enough cornstarch paste to thicken, stirring constantly.

7 Return the salmon to the wok and gently combine everything. Sprinkle with the green onion.

Serves 3 to 4

puffed rice noodles

Pour ½ cup (125 mL) vegetable oil into a skillet and heat on high heat until almost smoking. Add 1 cup (250 mL) rice vermicelli. Cook until the noodles puff up like popcorn, about 30 seconds.

Serves 3 to 4

grilled salmon with ginger orange butter

An easy, quick recipe. Use lime or lemon instead of orange if desired. Serve with asparagus and Minted New Potatoes (see page 129).

ginger orange butter

½ cup	butter, at room temperature	125 mL
1 tbsp	grated fresh ginger	15 mL
	Grated rind and juice of ½ orange	

1	1½-lb (750 g) salmon fillet	1
1 tbsp	olive oil	15 mL
	Salt and freshly ground pepper to taste	

1 To make the ginger orange butter, in a food processor or by hand, cream together the butter, ginger, orange rind and juice. Refrigerate until needed.

2 With a sharp knife angled almost parallel to the skin, slice the salmon into slices ½ inch (1.25 cm) thick, starting at the thicker end.

3 Line a baking sheet with parchment paper or foil. Place the salmon on top. Brush with the oil and season with salt and pepper.

4 Broil the salmon for 3 minutes, or until white juices rise to the surface. Do not turn the salmon. Serve with a dab of ginger orange butter.

Serves 4

salmon peking style

Served like Peking duck, this dish is wonderful finger food. You can prewrap the lettuce leaves, but I prefer to let guests assemble their own. You can also serve the salmon already wrapped, as a first course. This dish can be served either warm or cold.

1	1-lb (500 g) salmon fillet	1

marinade

¼ cup	soy sauce	50 mL
1 tbsp	dry sherry	15 mL
1 tsp	liquid honey	5 mL
2 tsp	lemon juice	10 mL
1	clove garlic, minced	1
1 tbsp	grated fresh ginger	15 mL
1 tsp	Dijon mustard	5 mL
¼ tsp	freshly ground pepper	1 mL
16	leaves Boston lettuce	16
2 tbsp	hoisin sauce	25 mL
4	green onions, slivered	4

1 Remove the skin from the salmon and cut crosswise into slices ⅛ inch (3 mm) thick. Place the salmon in a large shallow dish.

2 To make the marinade, in a small bowl, mix together the soy sauce, sherry, honey, lemon juice, garlic, ginger, mustard and pepper. Pour the marinade over the salmon and marinate at room temperature for 15 minutes. Remove the salmon from the marinade; reserve the marinade.

3 Place the salmon on an oiled baking sheet and broil for 2 minutes; turn over, brush with the marinade and broil for 2 minutes on the second side. When white juices rise to the surface, the salmon is ready. Place the salmon slices in the centre of a serving platter.

4 Brush each lettuce leaf with ¼ tsp (1 mL) hoisin sauce and arrange around the salmon. Garnish the platter with green onions.

5 To serve, wrap a piece of salmon and a piece of green onion in a lettuce leaf.

Serves 4 to 6

sole

Sole is part of the flounder family. The thin small fillets of grey or lemon sole are more delicate and tastier than the large fillets.

baked sole with leeks

This pretty dish has the added benefit of being low in calories – 200 calories per serving.

2	leeks (dark-green leaves removed), thinly sliced	2
4	4-oz (125 g) sole fillets	4
2 tsp	grated orange rind	10 mL
1 tsp	dried tarragon	5 mL
¼ tsp	salt	1 mL
	Freshly ground pepper to taste	
2 tbsp	orange juice	25 mL
½ cup	chicken stock	125mL
2 tbsp	butter	5 mL

1 Preheat the oven to 350° F (180° C).

2 Place half the leeks in an ungreased ovenproof baking dish. Top with the sole and remaining leeks.

3 Sprinkle with orange rind, tarragon, salt and pepper. Pour the orange juice and stock over top.

4 Cover the dish with foil and bake for 10 minutes, or until the sole is opaque.

5 Pour the liquid and leeks into a skillet. Bring to a boil and reduce until ¼ cup (50 mL) of liquid remains. Remove from the heat and stir in the butter. Pour over the sole and serve immediately.

Serves 4

red snapper florida style

A quick and easy recipe that tastes of the Florida sun. Try making it with shrimp, sole or sea bass.

2	8-oz (250 g) red snapper fillets	2
2 tbsp	olive oil	25 mL
1 tsp	dried thyme	5 mL
½ cup	chopped green onion	125 mL
1	clove garlic, minced	1
2 tbsp	finely chopped parsley	25 mL
¼ cup	fresh breadcrumbs	50 mL
	Salt and freshly ground pepper to taste	
1 tbsp	butter	15 mL
	Juice of 1 orange	

1 Preheat the oven to 450° F (230° F).
2 Place the snapper fillets in an oiled baking dish.
3 In a small bowl, combine the olive oil, thyme, green onion, garlic, parsley, breadcrumbs, salt and pepper. Sprinkle the mixture over the fish. Dot with the butter.
4 Pour the orange juice around the fish. Cover the dish with foil or parchment paper and bake for 10 minutes, or until white juices rise to the surface.
Serves 2

red snapper with lemon garlic sauce

This classic method of frying fish can also be used with trout, sole or pickerel fillets.

¼ cup	milk	50 mL
¼ cup	all-purpose flour	50 mL
	Salt and freshly ground pepper to taste	
4	8-oz (250 g) red snapper fillets	4
¼ cup	vegetable oil	50 mL
⅓ cup	butter	75 mL
2	cloves garlic, minced	2
3 tbsp	lemon juice	45 mL
3 tbsp	finely chopped parsley	45 mL

1 Pour the milk into a shallow bowl. Place the flour, salt and pepper in a dish. Dip the fish into the milk, then the flour.
2 In a large skillet, heat the oil over medium-high heat. Add the fish and cook for 90 seconds, or until golden-brown on 1 side. Turn over and repeat.
3 Remove the fish to a serving platter and discard all the oil. Add the butter to the skillet and cook until it begins to turn hazelnut-brown. Add the garlic, lemon juice and parsley. Cook for 30 seconds. Pour over the fish just before serving.
Serves 4

red snapper papillote

This recipe has overtones of the south of France. It always makes an elegant presentation because you cut the foil open with a flourish at the table so the colourful contents spill out. If fennel seeds are unavailable, use dried tarragon.

2 tbsp	olive oil	25 mL
2	8-oz (250 g) red snapper fillets	2
1 tsp	fennel seeds, crushed	5 mL
¼ tsp	cayenne pepper	1 mL
2	leeks (dark-green leaves removed), coarsely chopped	2
2	cloves garlic, thinly sliced	2
2	tomatoes, peeled, seeded and chopped	2
	Salt and freshly ground pepper to taste	
2 tbsp	dry white wine	25 mL

1 Preheat the oven to 450° F (230° C).

2 Place 2 12-inch (30 cm) square sheets of foil on the counter. Sprinkle with 1 tbsp (15 mL) olive oil. Lay a fillet on half of each square. Sprinkle with the fennel and cayenne.

3 Heat the remaining oil in a skillet on medium-high heat. Sauté the leeks until limp, about 2 minutes. Add the garlic and tomatoes. Sauté until the sauce is heated through, 1 to 2 minutes. Season with salt and pepper and spread over the fish.

Sprinkle with the wine.

4 Fold the second half of the foil over, crimping the edges together.

5 Place the packages on a baking sheet and bake for 10 to 12 minutes, or until the packages puff. Serve the packages on plates, cutting them open at the table.

Serves 2

red snapper

Red snapper is a sweet, firm-fleshed fish that is delicious barbecued, poached or sautéed. It is sold whole or in fillets.

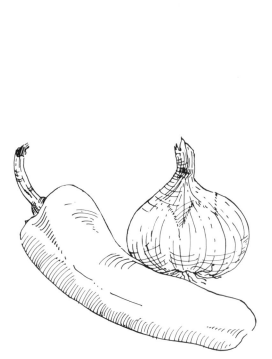

baked fish steaks

A simple, elegant baked fish with a sauce enriched with whipping cream. Use any kind of fish steaks such as grouper or halibut. Serve with rice or plain boiled potatoes.

½ cup	chopped onion	125 mL
½ cup	chopped carrot	125 mL
½ cup	chopped celery	125 mL
4	6-oz (180 g) fish steaks	4
1	bay leaf	1
¼ tsp	dried thyme	1 mL
¼ cup	dry white wine	50 mL
⅓ cup	whipping cream	75 mL
¼ cup	finely chopped parsley	50 mL
	Salt and freshly ground pepper to taste	

1 Preheat the oven to 400° F (200° C).
2 Sprinkle the vegetables on an ungreased baking dish large enough to hold the fish in 1 layer. Place the fish steaks on top. Add the bay leaf, thyme and wine.
3 Bake, covered, for 10 minutes, or until white juices rise to the surface.
4 Reserve the fish and strain the liquid into a pot. Bring to a boil. Add the whipping cream and boil for 2 to 3 minutes, or until the sauce thickens slightly.
5 Stir in the parsley and season to taste. Pour the sauce over the fish before serving.
Serves 4

grilled swordfish or tuna

This method of grilling firm-fleshed fish works beautifully. By heating the baking sheet before placing the fish on it, you cook it underneath while broiling it on top, eliminating the need to turn the fish over. Try serving this with Sun-dried Tomato Salsa.

2 tbsp	olive oil	25 mL
2 tbsp	chopped fresh tarragon, thyme or rosemary, or 2 tsp (10 mL) dried	25 mL
1½ lb	swordfish or tuna steaks	750 g
2 tbsp	balsamic vinegar	25 mL
	Salt and freshly ground pepper to taste	

1 In a small bowl, combine the oil and herb. Brush over the swordfish steaks.
2 Preheat the broiler and heat an ungreased baking sheet under it for 5 minutes. Place the fish on the hot baking sheet and broil for 4 to 5 minutes, or until firm to the touch. Do not turn the fish over.
3 Place the fish on a serving platter. Drizzle with balsamic vinegar. Season with salt and pepper.
Serves 4

sun-dried tomato salsa

A good salsa to accompany grilled sword-fish or tuna. Finely chop ½ cup (125 mL) sun-dried tomatoes, ½ cup (125 mL) black olives, 2 cloves garlic and 1 tbsp (15 mL) fresh basil. Combine and stir in 2 tbsp (25 mL) olive oil and 1 tsp (5 mL) red wine vinegar. Season with salt and freshly ground pepper to taste.

Makes about 1 cup (250 mL)

grilled halibut with tomato herb vinaigrette

Halibut is a lean firm-fleshed fish with lots of taste. Often the fish will weigh up to 100 lb (50 kg) when caught. Use grouper or swordfish instead of halibut, if desired.

4	6-oz (180 g) halibut steaks	4
2 tbsp	lemon juice	25 mL
1 tbsp	olive oil	15 mL
1 tsp	finely chopped rosemary, or	5 mL
	½ tsp (2 mL) dried	
	Salt and freshly	
	ground pepper to taste	

tomato herb vinaigrette

½ cup	diced ripe tomato	125 mL
¼ cup	coarsely chopped fresh basil	50 mL
	or parsley	
2 tbsp	chopped green onion	25 mL
1 tbsp	red wine vinegar	15 mL
2 tbsp	olive oil	25 mL
	Salt and freshly	
	ground pepper to taste	

1 Place the halibut steaks in a dish large enough to hold the fish in a single layer.
2 In a small bowl, combine the lemon juice, 1 tbsp (15 mL) oil, rosemary, salt and pepper. Pour over halibut, turning to coat both sides. Marinate at room temperature for 30 minutes.
3 Preheat the broiler and heat an un-greased baking sheet under it for 5 minutes. Place the fish on the hot baking sheet and broil for 4 to 5 minutes, or until the fish is opaque. Do not turn the fish over.
4 Meanwhile, in a small bowl, combine the tomato, basil, green onion, vinegar and 2 tbsp (25 mL) oil. Whisk together until blended. Season with salt and pepper.
5 Spoon the vinaigrette over each steak before serving.

Serves 4

51

roasted monkfish with red wine glaze

The pristine monkfish sitting in a pool of burgundy sauce looks wonderful on a plain white dinner plate. Use this special recipe for a dinner party and serve it with steamed rice and Cumin-scented Spinach (see page 131).

1½ lb	monkfish fillets	750 g
1 tsp	dried thyme	5 mL
2 tbsp	olive oil	25 mL
½ cup	orange juice	125 mL
1 tbsp	granulated sugar	15 mL
½ cup	dry red wine	125 mL
1 tbsp	red wine vinegar	15 mL
1 tsp	tomato paste	5 mL
2 tbsp	butter	25 mL

1 Preheat the oven to 400° F (200° C).
2 Trim the monkfish of all sinew. Place the fish in an ovenproof baking dish. Sprinkle with the thyme and olive oil.
3 Bake, uncovered, for 15 minutes, or until white juices rise to the surface.
4 Meanwhile, in a pot, combine the orange juice, sugar, wine, vinegar and tomato paste. Bring to a boil and boil, uncovered, until the liquid reduces to ⅓ cup (75 mL), about 3 minutes. Add any accumulated juices from the monkfish and bring to a boil again.
5 Remove the pot from the heat and whisk in the butter. The sauce should be slightly thick and glossy.
6 Slice the monkfish into slices about ¼ inch (5 mm) thick and serve with a spoonful of the glaze.
   Serves 4

smoked fish hash

Ben Geneen, my father, loves rich flavours. My mother, Pearl, concocted this recipe to give a whole new meaning to the word hash. The recipe is made along the same lines as corned beef hash, but it is lighter, spicier and much more interesting. Use one kind of smoked fish or a mixture of several. Top with a poached egg, if desired.

2 tbsp	butter	25 mL
1	small onion, chopped	1
8 oz	mushrooms, sliced	250 g
2 tbsp	all-purpose flour	25 mL
1 tbsp	grated lemon rind	15 mL
1 tsp	curry powder	5 mL
1 cup	milk	250 mL
1	bay leaf	1
¼ cup	light cream	50 mL
4 oz	smoked salmon, chopped	125 g

4 oz	smoked trout, chopped	125 g
4 oz	kippers, chopped	125 g
2 tbsp	finely chopped parsley	25 mL
	Salt and freshly ground pepper to taste	
4	slices toast	4

1 In a large skillet, heat the butter on high heat until it sizzles. Add the onion and sauté until softened slightly, about 2 minutes.

2 Add the mushrooms and sauté until they are limp. Sprinkle in the flour, lemon rind and curry powder. Cook together, stirring, until the flour and butter are incorporated.

3 Add the milk and bay leaf. Bring to a boil, stirring. Turn the heat to low and stir in the cream.

4 In a small bowl, combine the smoked salmon, smoked trout and kippers. Stir the fish into the sauce. Cook until heated through. Add the parsley and season well with salt and pepper.

5 Place 1 slice of toast on each plate and top with the hash.

Serves 4

grilled scallops

These herb-infused scallops are great in the summer right off the barbecue. If you don't have a special fish grill to stop the scallops from falling through the grilling rack, place them on skewers first. Use this marinade with other fish, too.

Try serving this dish with Warm Noodle Salad (see page 118).

herb marinade

1 tsp	finely chopped green chili	5 mL
2 tbsp	finely chopped fresh basil	25 mL
2 tbsp	vegetable oil	25 mL
12	large scallops	12

1 To make the marinade, combine the chili, basil and oil in a bowl. Add the scallops and marinate for 30 minutes at room temperature.

2 Remove the scallops from the marinade and grill or broil for 2 minutes on each side, or until they are firm to the touch.

Serves 4

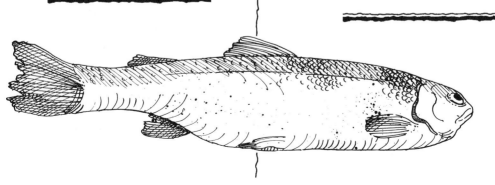

sautéed spicy scallops

Wear rubber gloves when seeding a chili, for its strong oil can burn the skin. As chilies vary in heat (often the smallest are the most lethal), start with half a chili, adding more if you want a hotter flavour.

2 tbsp	olive oil	25 mL
2	cloves garlic, finely chopped	2
2 tbsp	finely chopped fresh ginger	25 mL
1	fresh green or red chili, seeded and finely chopped	1
½	red pepper, thinly sliced	½
12 oz	scallops	375 g
½ cup	fish or chicken stock	125 mL
¼ cup	butter	50 mL
1 tbsp	finely chopped fresh coriander or mint	15 mL

1 In a large skillet, heat the oil on high heat. Sauté the garlic, ginger, chili and red pepper for 20 seconds.

2 Toss in the scallops and cook, stirring frequently, for 2 to 3 minutes, or until the scallops are firm to the touch. Remove the scallops.

3 Add the stock to the skillet and bring to a boil. Cook, stirring occasionally, until reduced to ¼ cup (50 mL), about 3 minutes.

4 Reduce the heat to low and swirl in the butter. Return the scallops to the skillet and simmer for 1 minute to heat through. Sprinkle with the coriander and serve immediately.

Serves 4

scallops

Scallops come in many different sizes, ranging from the large sea scallops to the tiny bay ones. The bay scallops have a more delicate flavour. Try to buy scallops fresh because the frozen ones tend to be watery. If they are the only ones available, defrost them in the refrigerator overnight and pat dry before using. Before cooking scallops, remove the tough little muscle on the rim where the meat was attached to the shell.

oysters

When buying oysters, look for ones that feel heavy in your hand. The top shell should be rounded. If the oysters are very fresh, they should keep for up to one week if refrigerated and covered with a wet cloth. An easy method of opening an oyster is to pop it into the microwave for 20 seconds to loosen its shell, or bake in a 400° F (200° C) oven for 2 minutes.

bruce's deep-fried oysters

My husband, Bruce, frequently requests this dish because he loves oysters. Already shucked oysters are available, fresh and frozen, at seafood counters in Chinese supermarkets. If you cannot find shucked oysters, use peeled shrimp, scallops or chicken. If the oysters are the large Pacific ones, cut them in half after blanching. If you use the smaller Malpeque oysters, buy sixteen. You can blanch and deep-fry the oysters and prepare the sauce ahead of time to make the final cooking easy. Serve these with rice and stir-fried broccoli.

seasoning sauce

½ cup	chicken stock	125 mL
1 tbsp	oyster sauce	15 mL
pinch	salt	pinch
pinch	granulated sugar	pinch
1 tsp	soy sauce	5 mL
1 tsp	sesame oil	5 mL
1 tsp	cornstarch mixed with 1 tsp (5 mL) water	5 mL
8	Pacific oysters, shucked, or 16 smaller ones	8
½ cup	cornstarch	125 mL
	Vegetable oil for deep-frying	

1	clove garlic, finely chopped	1
6	thin slices peeled fresh ginger, slivered	6
4	green onions, slivered	4
2 cups	shredded iceberg lettuce	500 mL

1 In a small bowl, combine all the ingredients for the seasoning sauce.

2 Bring a large pot of water to a boil. Add the oysters and boil for 30 seconds to blanch. Remove and drain well.

3 Coat the oysters with ½ cup (125 mL) cornstarch, shaking off the excess.

4 In a wok or large skillet on high heat, heat 2 inches (5 cm) oil. When it is very hot (a cube of bread should turn brown in 20 seconds), add the oysters. Deep-fry until golden brown, 1 to 2 minutes. Remove and drain on paper towels. Pour off all but 1 tbsp (15 mL) oil.

5 Add the garlic, ginger and green onions to the oil and stir-fry for 30 seconds.

6 Pour in the prepared seasoning sauce. Bring to a boil, stirring. Add the oysters to the sauce, stir and heat through. Serve on a bed of lettuce.

Serves 4

cajun shrimp

With the recent interest in regional cooking and the excellent public relations skills of Paul Prudhomme and his K. Paul's restaurant in New Orleans, the spicy, lusty food of Louisiana has become popular in Canada.

⅓ cup	vegetable oil	75 mL
⅓ cup	all-purpose flour	75 mL
¼ cup	chopped onion	50 mL
¼ cup	chopped celery	50 mL
¼ cup	chopped green pepper	50 mL
1 tsp	cayenne pepper	5 mL
1 tsp	dried thyme	5 mL
pinch	paprika	pinch
3 cups	chicken stock	750 mL
¼ cup	butter	50 mL
1½ lb	large shrimp, peeled	750 g
1 cup	chopped green onion	250 mL
1	clove garlic, chopped	1

1 Heat the oil on high heat in a large pot. Whisk in the flour and cook, whisking, until the flour is dark-brown, about 3 minutes. Remove from the heat.

2 Stir the onion, celery, green pepper, cayenne, thyme and paprika into the flour mixture. Stir until the vegetables soften slightly, 2 to 3 minutes. Return to the heat and add the stock. Bring to a boil, stirring.

3 Reduce the heat to medium-low and simmer, uncovered, for about 5 minutes, or until the floury taste has disappeared.

4 In a large skillet, melt the butter on medium heat. Sauté the shrimp, green onion and garlic until the shrimp begins to turn pink, about 2 minutes. Add the sauce. Continue to cook for 5 minutes longer, or until the shrimp is cooked through.

Serves 6

preparing shrimp

To peel and devein shrimp, detach the shell by pulling off the legs. Then grasp the shell between your thumb and forefinger and push it off. Deveining shrimp is not necessary, but if you feel you must, then with a sharp knife cut along the outer curve of the body and the vein will come away.

To butterfly shrimp, slice through the body along the outside curve, but stop short of cutting right through. Open the shrimp so that it lies flat.

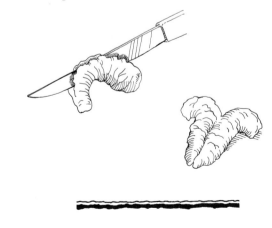

low-country muddle

Shrimp is a traditional ingredient in this recipe from South Carolina. Shrimp retain more flavour if they are cooked in their shells. The taste is even better, too, when the muddle is boiled on the barbecue and eaten outside. This is a great dish to serve when you are entertaining lots of people. Just keep adding more shrimp, corn and Polish sausage. Serve this with Jalapeño Lime Butter.

1 lb	large shrimp, in the shell	500 g
1 lb	smoked sausage or	500 g
	Polish sausage	
4	ears corn, shucked	4
12 cups	water	3 L
2	bay leaves	2
1 tbsp	chopped fresh thyme, or	15 mL
	1 tsp (5 mL) dried	
1 tsp	chili powder	5 mL
1 tsp	dried oregano	5 mL
1 tsp	cayenne pepper	5 mL
1 tbsp	whole peppercorns	15 mL
2 tsp	salt	10 mL

1 Wash the shrimp. Slice the sausage into chunks. Cut each ear of corn into thirds.
2 Bring a large pot of water to a boil. Sprinkle in the bay leaves, thyme, chili powder, oregano, cayenne, peppercorns and salt. Boil for 2 minutes.

3 Add the sausage to the pot and boil for 5 minutes. Add the corn and boil for 2 minutes. Add the shrimp and boil until pink and curled, about 3 minutes.
4 Drain the sausage, corn and shrimp and pile on a large serving platter.
Serves 6 to 8

jalapeño lime butter

Serve this butter with Low-Country Muddle or with grilled shrimp. It can also be spread on biscuits. If you using canned jalapeño peppers, rinse them first. The butter can be frozen for up to two months.

In a small bowl, combine ¼ cup (50 mL) soft butter, 1 tsp (5 mL) finely chopped jalapeño pepper (or more to taste), 1 tsp (5 mL) lime juice and 1 tsp (5 mL) grated lime rind. Refrigerate until needed.

Makes about ¼ cup (50 mL)

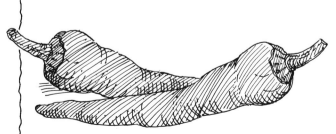

fresh and spicy shrimp curry

The sharp taste of vinegar balances the hot chilies in this dish. If less heat is desired, remove the seeds from the chilies before chopping. Serve with steamed rice and Pungent Eggplant (see page 126).

2 tsp	ground cumin	10 mL
1 tsp	dried chili flakes	5 mL
¼ cup	rice or wine vinegar	50 mL
3 tbsp	vegetable oil	45 mL
1	Spanish onion, chopped	1
1 tbsp	finely chopped fresh ginger	15 mL
4	cloves garlic, finely chopped	4
2 tbsp	finely chopped fresh coriander	25 mL
1 tsp	turmeric	5 mL
½ cup	chopped canned tomatoes	125 mL
1 lb	large shrimp, peeled and butterflied	500 g
	Salt and freshly ground pepper to taste	

1 In a small bowl or measuring cup, combine the cumin, chili flakes and 2 tbsp (25 mL) vinegar. Reserve.
2 Heat the oil in a large skillet on low heat and cook the onion for 10 minutes, stirring occasionally. Add the ginger and garlic, cooking and stirring for a further 10 minutes, or until very soft and slightly coloured.
3 Add the coriander, turmeric and vinegar mixture. Stir for 1 minute. Stir in the tomato, increase the heat to high and bring to a boil.
4 Add the shrimp and cook until pink and curled, about 3 minutes.
5 Pour in the remaining 2 tbsp (25 mL) vinegar and season with salt and pepper.
Serves 3

moules marinières

A simple supper dish – easy to make and easy on the pocketbook. Serve the mussels with plenty of French bread for dipping.

2	onions, chopped	2
2 tsp	dried thyme	10 mL
4	cloves garlic, thinly sliced	4
1 tsp	freshly ground pepper	5 mL
1 cup	dry white wine	250 mL
1 cup	water	250 mL
2 lb	mussels, cleaned	1 kg

1 Place the onions in the bottom of a large pot. Add the thyme, garlic, pepper, wine and water. On high heat, bring to a boil and boil for 3 minutes.
2 Add the mussels, cover and cook until the mussels open, 3 to 5 minutes. Remove the mussels as they open. Before serving, pour the liquid over the mussels.
Serves 4

Do-it-yourself tostadas, page 25

Bruschetta, page 27

Salad pizza, page 27

Cream of sweet potato soup, page 32

Poached salmon fillets, page 44

Red snapper with lemon garlic sauce, page 48

Lemon-scented chicken, page 72

Aromatic beef with pinot noir sauce, page 84

mussels

Make sure mussels are tightly closed when you buy them. If they are open and don't close when you tap them, the mussels are dead and should be thrown out. If the mussels don't open when they are steamed, they died before they were cooked and should not be eaten.

Before cooking mussels, remove the beards (the feathery hairs sprouting from the shell). Mussels can be kept for up to three days covered with a towel in the coldest part of the refrigerator.

seafood ragout

A cross between a soup and a stew, this quick, easy dish is perfect for a light supper. If fish stock is unavailable, use chicken stock. Serve the ragout topped with Fresh Basil Rouille.

2	leeks (dark-green leaves removed), sliced	2
1	carrot, sliced	1
1	stalk celery, chopped	1
2	cloves garlic, thinly sliced	2
1	bay leaf	1
½ cup	dry white wine	125 mL
1½ cups	fish stock	375 mL
2	tomatoes, chopped	2
1 lb	mussels, cleaned	500 g
8 oz	shrimp, peeled	250 g
8 oz	scallops	250 g

1 In a large pot on medium heat, combine half the leeks with the carrot, celery, garlic, bay leaf, wine, stock and tomatoes. Simmer for 20 minutes.

2 Raise the heat to high, bring to a boil and toss in the mussels. Boil until the mussels open, 2 to 4 minutes. Remove them from the pot with tongs, cool slightly, then remove the meat from the shells. Discard any mussels that do not open.

3 Strain the stock, pressing the vegetables lightly to release flavours. Return the stock to the pot and reduce the heat to low.

4 Add the shrimp, scallops and remaining leeks to the stock; simmer until the shrimp are pink and curled, about 3 minutes.

5 Return the mussels to the pot and reheat. Divide the ragout among 4 soup bowls.
Serves 4

fresh basil rouille

This rouille is excellent with fish, grilled chicken or swirled into hearty soups. Combine ¼ cup (50 mL) finely chopped fresh basil with 1 chopped tomato. Season well with a pinch of cayenne, salt and pepper. Whisk in 2 tbsp (25 mL) olive oil.

Makes about ½ cup (125 mL)

shellfish medley with lemon butter sauce

A dynamite first course or main dish that can be cooked quickly on the barbecue or under the broiler. The sauce can also be served with steamed vegetables, fried fish or veal scallops.

12	large shrimp, in the shell	12
24	mussels, cleaned	24
12	clams, cleaned	12

lemon butter sauce

½ cup	butter	125 mL
1 tbsp	lemon juice	15 mL
	Salt and freshly ground pepper to taste	

Lemon wedges

1 Butterfly the shrimp through the backs, leaving the shells on.

2 Barbecue or broil the shrimp, mussels and clams. Turn the shrimp as they begin to curl and remove them when they are pink and curled. Remove the mussels and clams from the grill as soon as the shells open. (If any do not open, discard them.) The total grilling time should be about 5 minutes.

3 Meanwhile, to make the sauce, melt the butter in a small pot over medium heat. Mix in the lemon juice, salt and pepper.

4 Serve the seafood with the sauce, garnished with lemon wedges.

Serves 2 as a main course; serves 4 as an appetizer

quick tips for leftover fish or seafood

- If you want to keep cooked fish for longer than 24 hours, make a marinade of lemon juice and oil and pour it over the fish. This should keep it fresh for up to three days.

- Combine leftover fish or seafood with a thick white sauce made from butter, flour and milk. Season well with salt and pepper and use as an omelette or crêpe filling.

- Make a spicy tomato sauce, fold in cooked fish at the last minute and serve with pasta.

- To make a fish or seafood mousse, process cooked fish or seafood with a couple of spoonfuls of butter and enough whipping cream to make a spreading consistency. Season well with salt and pepper and serve with cucumber slices and toast.

chapter five

CHICKEN & DUCK

*C*hicken is the mainstay of the faster food cook. It's readily
available, reasonably priced and cooks quickly using all sorts
of cooking techniques. Chicken can also be adapted to a wide range
of tastes and cuisines; because of its versatility, you could make
chicken every day for a year and never repeat a recipe. Chicken is
also lower in calories than meat, and it has a lower fat content.

61

tips

- You can buy chicken whole or cut in pieces. Chicken parts are convenient for the cook in a hurry because they cook more quickly than whole chickens.
- Chicken breasts are always popular, although I don't think they are as flavourful or juicy as legs and thighs. You can buy breasts with the bone and skin on, boneless skinless breasts or, occasionally, boneless breasts with the skin left on.
- Battery-raised white-skinned supermarket chicken doesn't have a lot of flavour. If you can find them, the more expensive free-range chickens have much more taste.
- After buying chicken, remove it from any plastic wrapping and store it loosely wrapped in waxed paper or covered with a paper towel in the meat drawer of the refrigerator.
- Chicken on the bone goes off faster than boneless chicken, so try to use it within one day. If you have to keep it for a few days, rub the exposed bones with lemon juice to help prevent the chicken from going off.
- It is the chicken skin that contains most of the fat, but the skin also gives chicken much of its flavour. If you want to remove the skin, do so after the chicken is cooked.
- Cooked chicken usually freezes well; uncooked chicken tends to lose flavour in the freezer.
- You can often find duck cut in pieces like chicken. If you buy a whole duck, cut it up before cooking for the best results.

easy grilled chicken

A quick grill that can be served alone or with a dab of Aioli (see page 10) or Pesto Butter (see page 71). Accompany with Scalloped Tomatoes (see page 132) or sliced fresh tomatoes.

1 tsp	dried tarragon	5 mL
1 tsp	dried rosemary	5 mL
	Grated rind and juice of 1 lime	
1 tbsp	Dijon mustard	15 mL
2 tbsp	olive oil	25 mL
4	single boneless chicken breasts	4

1 In a small bowl, combine the tarragon, rosemary, lime rind and juice, mustard and olive oil.

2 Brush the oil mixture on both sides of the chicken breasts and place on a baking sheet.

3 Broil the chicken for about 5 minutes per side, or until the chicken is golden and the juices run clear.

Serves 4

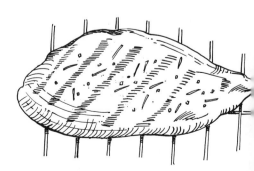

instant aioli

Instant aioli can be made by combining 1/2 cup (125 mL) commercial mayonnaise with 1 minced clove garlic. Add lemon juice to taste.

stir-fried chicken with vegetables

A light, low-cal stir-fry with lots of vegetables. Serve with steamed rice. Substitute shrimp or pork for the chicken, if desired.

2 cups	broccoli florets	500 mL
1	red pepper, diced	1
4 oz	snow peas, trimmed	125 g
1/2 cup	chicken stock	125 mL
2 tsp	cornstarch	10 mL
1 tbsp	dry white wine	15 mL
2 tbsp	soy sauce	25 mL
1 tsp	granulated sugar	5 mL
1 tbsp	vegetable oil	15 mL
3 tbsp	finely chopped fresh ginger	45 mL
1	clove garlic, finely chopped	1
1 tsp	dried chili flakes, optional	5 mL
1 lb	boneless chicken, skin removed, cubed	500 g
8 oz	mushrooms, sliced	250 g
1 tsp	sesame oil	5 mL

1 Bring a large pot water to a boil. Add the broccoli and red pepper. Boil for 30 seconds, add the snow peas and continue to boil for another 30 seconds. Drain and rinse the vegetables with cold water. Reserve.

2 In a small bowl, combine the chicken stock, cornstarch, wine, soy sauce and sugar. Stir until smooth.

3 Heat the oil in a wok or large skillet over high heat. Add the ginger, garlic and chili flakes. Stir-fry for 30 seconds. Add the chicken and stir-fry for about 3 minutes, or until the chicken is cooked through.

4 Add the mushrooms and stir-fry with the chicken for 1 minute. Add the blanched vegetables.

5 Stir the reserved sauce together and pour over the chicken. Bring to a boil, stirring until the sauce thickens. Stir in the sesame oil. Serve immediately.

Serves 4

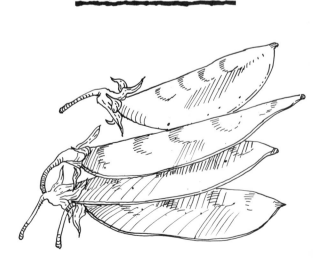

sautéed chicken with spiced orange sauce

A summery chicken dish. The sauce is great with barbecued chicken wings, too. Serve it in small bowls for dipping, with Savoury Couscous (see page 102) alongside.

4	**single boneless chicken breasts, skin removed**	4
½ cup	**orange juice**	125 mL
1 tbsp	**brandy**	15 mL
1 tsp	**grated orange rind**	5 mL
pinch	**ground cardamom**	pinch
¼ cup	**chopped fresh mint**	50 mL
2 tbsp	**all-purpose flour**	25 mL
	Salt and freshly ground pepper to taste	
2 tbsp	**olive oil**	25 mL
½ cup	**chicken stock**	125 mL

1 Pound the chicken breasts until they are an even ½-inch (1.25 cm) thickness.
2 In a flat dish, mix together the orange juice, brandy, orange rind, cardamom and 2 tbsp (25 mL) mint to form a marinade.
3 In a second flat dish, season the flour with salt and pepper. Dip the chicken into the marinade, then dredge in the flour. Reserve marinade.
4 In a large skillet, heat the oil over medium-high heat. Add the chicken and cook for 5 minutes on each side, or until golden-brown and cooked through. Remove the breasts and pour off the fat.
5 Add the marinade and chicken stock to the skillet. Bring to a boil and cook for about 5 minutes, or until reduced to about ½ cup (125 mL). Season with salt and pepper. Return the chicken breasts to the pan to rewarm and sprinkle with the remaining 2 tbsp (25 mL) mint.

Serves 4

arrowroot and cornstarch

Arrowroot is the tasteless, finely ground root of a tropical plant. It gets its name from the fact that it was used by the natives of tropical countries to heal arrow wounds! It is a better thickener than cornstarch because it produces a clear, limpid sauce that is not gluey. Arrowroot does not have to be boiled in order to thicken a sauce; it only needs to be brought to a simmer.

Cornstarch and arrowroot can be used interchangeably. Cornstarch is traditionally used in Oriental recipes, but it must come to a boil to remove its taste. Both arrowroot and cornstarch should be combined with at least equal amounts of liquid and mixed to a paste before being added to the sauce.

To pound chicken or veal to an even thickness, place the meat between two sheets of waxed paper and pound it with a mallet or the bottom of a heavy pot.

caribbean chicken breasts

Serve this easy, fresh-tasting recipe with rice combined with orange rind and almonds and steamed Cumin-scented Spinach (see page 131).

1 cup	orange juice	250 mL
	Grated rind and juice of 1 lime	
¼ cup	finely chopped parsley	50 mL
1 tbsp	dry mustard	15 mL
1	clove garlic, minced	1
3 tbsp	soy sauce	45 mL
3 tbsp	liquid honey	45 mL
1 tsp	salt	5 mL
½ tsp	dried chili flakes, optional	2 mL
2 tbsp	olive oil	25 mL
6	single boneless chicken breasts	6

1 In a bowl, combine all the ingredients except the chicken breasts. Add the breasts, spoon the sauce over and marinate at room temperature for 15 minutes.
2 Remove the chicken from the marinade and broil or grill for 5 minutes. Baste with the marinade, turn and broil for 5 minutes, or until the juices run clear.
3 While the breasts are cooking, add the remaining marinade to a pot, bring to a boil and reduce until ½ cup (125 mL) remains. Skim off any scum. Serve spooned over the chicken breasts.
Serves 4 to 6

southern fried chicken

Southern fried chicken is one of my basic comfort foods. I love the crisp outer coating and the juicy interior. I learned to fry chicken from Natalie Dupree, a great Southern cook, and her method always turns out a superior dish. The chicken is crusty and juicy and, because it is deep-fried at a high temperature, it does not become greasy. If you are serving a lot of people, make the chicken ahead and reheat it in a 350° F (180° C) oven, uncovered, for 20 minutes, or until hot. You can also make this recipe with boneless chicken breasts cut in strips, for homemade chicken nuggets. Serve with Buttermilk Biscuits (see page 159).

1	**3-lb (1.5 kg) chicken, cut into 8 pieces**	**1**
2 cups	**shortening or vegetable oil, approx.**	**500 mL**
	Salt and freshly ground pepper to taste	
1 cup	**all-purpose flour**	**250 mL**

1 Rinse the chicken and place in a colander.

2 Melt the shortening in a 12-inch (30 cm) skillet on high heat, making sure the skillet is no more than half full.

3 Salt and pepper the chicken. Place the flour in a plastic bag or on a baking sheet.

4 Coat the still-damp chicken with the flour. Knock off the excess. Coat again and knock off the excess flour.

5 When the shortening reaches 360° F (182° C), or when a cube of bread turns brown in 30 seconds, add the chicken to the skillet, in batches if necessary, skin side down. Add the dark meat first in the centre of the skillet and surround with the white meat. The pieces can touch, but don't crowd the skillet. Cover loosely.

6 Turn the heat to medium-high and cook for 9 to 10 minutes, or until dark golden. Turn the chicken and cook for 8 to 10 minutes more, uncovered. Drain it on paper towels.

Serves 4

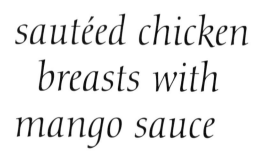

sautéed chicken breasts with mango sauce

This piquant chicken dish is excellent for a buffet because you don't need a knife to eat it. This recipe has good depth of flavour but is not spicily hot. If you do not have mango chutney, any chutney will do. Garnish with slices of mango or orange and serve with rice. The recipe can be doubled or tripled. You can make this up to three days ahead, refrigerate it and reheat at

350° F (180° C) for 20 minutes, or until the sauce is bubbling hot.

8	single boneless chicken breasts, skin removed	8
3 tbsp	vegetable oil	45 mL
1	large onion, chopped	1
3	cloves garlic, finely chopped	3
2 tbsp	finely chopped fresh ginger	25 mL
1 tbsp	curry powder	15 mL
½ cup	mango chutney	125 mL
2 cups	chicken stock	500 mL
½ cup	desiccated coconut	125 mL
1 tbsp	tomato paste	15 mL
1 tbsp	lemon juice	15 mL
	Salt and freshly ground pepper to taste	
2 tbsp	finely chopped fresh coriander or parsley	25 mL

1 Slice the chicken breasts into 1-inch (2.5 cm) cubes.

2 Heat the oil in a large skillet on medium heat. Sauté the onion, garlic, ginger and curry powder until the onion softens, about 2 minutes.

3 Add the chicken cubes and stir until coated with the spices. Mix in the chutney, chicken stock, coconut and tomato paste. Bring to a boil; reduce the heat to medium-low and simmer, uncovered, for 5 to 7 minutes, or until the chicken is cooked.

4 Add the lemon juice, salt and pepper and simmer together for 5 minutes longer to combine the flavours. Sprinkle with coriander before serving.

Serves 8

curry powder

Commercial curry powder is unknown in India because each household grinds its own particular blend of whole spices for each dish. Commercial curry powder is a ready-to-use mixture of spices such as turmeric, coriander, cumin, cayenne, cinnamon, cardamom, cloves, ginger and mustard seed. It is finely ground and often lacking in any real flavour. The following mixture can be made at home and keeps for about six months. I add cayenne or chilies to taste, depending on what dish I am making.

In a coffee grinder or blender, grind 2 tbsp (25 mL) coriander seeds, 1 tbsp (15 mL) cardamom seeds, 2 tbsp (25 mL) cumin seeds, 1 tbsp (15 mL) black peppercorns, 1 tbsp (15 mL) whole cloves and 2 2-inch (5 cm) cinnamon sticks. Stir in 1 tsp (5 mL) ground turmeric. Store in a jar in a cupboard.

Makes about ½ cup (125 mL)

spicy portuguese chicken

This typical Portuguese recipe is equally delicious made with thinly sliced flank steak. I like it really spicy, but you can control the heat by adding less hot sauce or eliminating the banana peppers. Serve it on crusty Portuguese or Italian buns with a salad.

4	**single boneless chicken breasts**	4
3	**cloves garlic, minced**	3
1 cup	**tomato sauce**	250 mL
½ tsp	**Tabasco**	2 mL
2 tbsp	**barbecue sauce or chili sauce**	25 mL
	Salt and freshly ground pepper to taste	
2 tbsp	**vegetable oil**	25 mL
1 tsp	**butter**	5 mL
3	**hot pickled banana peppers, slivered**	3

1 Cut the chicken breasts into 1-inch (2.5 cm) strips. Set aside.

2 In a large bowl, combine the garlic, tomato sauce, Tabasco, barbecue sauce, salt and pepper. Add the chicken and marinate at room temperature for 15 minutes.

3 Heat the oil and butter in a large skillet on high heat. Remove the chicken strips from the marinade; cook for 1 minute on each side, or until slightly browned. With a slotted spoon, remove from the pan.

4 Pour off the fat and add the marinade to the skillet. Bring to a boil and return the chicken strips. Lower the heat to medium. Sprinkle in the banana peppers. Simmer, uncovered, for 5 minutes, or until the chicken is cooked through.

Serves 4

goan chicken curry

A delicate curry that won't offend those who are not wild for chilies. If you like a hot curry, add more chilies. Many curries from the Goan region of India feature coconut milk and vinegar for a sweet/tart flavour. Serve with Coconut Spinach Rice (see page 109) and a tomato salad.

2 tbsp	vegetable oil	25 mL
1	large onion, finely chopped	1
3 tbsp	finely chopped fresh ginger	45 mL
6	cloves garlic, finely chopped	6
1	green chili, seeded and finely chopped, optional	1
2 tbsp	curry powder	25 mL
1 tbsp	turmeric	5 mL
4	single boneless chicken breasts, skin removed, sliced into 2-inch (5 cm) strips	4
	Grated rind and juice of 1 lime	
1	14-oz (400 mL) can coconut milk	1
1 tbsp	white vinegar	15 mL
	Salt to taste	
2 tbsp	finely chopped fresh coriander	25 mL

1 Heat the oil over medium-low heat in a wok or large skillet. Sauté the onion slowly until softened and browned on the edges, about 10 minutes. Add the ginger, garlic and chili. Sauté for 5 minutes longer.

2 Stir in the curry powder and turmeric and cook, stirring, until fragrant, about 1 minute. Add the chicken and sauté until it is coated with the spices.

3 Stir in the lime rind and juice, coconut milk and vinegar. Bring to a boil. Simmer for 10 to 15 minutes, or until the chicken is tender. Taste for seasoning, adding salt or more lime juice as needed. Sprinkle with the coriander just before serving.

Serves 4

coriander

Coriander, cilantro or Chinese parsley is the fragrant, flowery-tasting, lacy herb that is indigenous to Mexican, Indian and Asian cooking. It has recently acquired cult status in North American cuisine because of its distinctive flavour. It looks a bit like Italian parsley and can now be bought at many supermarkets. Coriander seeds are the seeds of the coriander plant, but they do not taste like the herb.

If you have inadvertently made a dish too spicy, stir in up to ½ cup (125 mL) plain yogourt or sour cream and 2 tbsp (25 mL) jam or chutney. Reheat the dish, but do not boil.

cheesy baked chicken

This recipe can be served plain, but the traditional cream gravy gives it added spark. The gravy can also be served with Southern Fried Chicken (see page 66). (If you use skinless chicken breasts, supplement the fat with butter to make the gravy.)

2 tbsp	all-purpose flour	25 mL
2 tbsp	grated Parmesan cheese	25 mL
1 tsp	dried basil	5 mL
pinch	cayenne pepper	pinch
	Salt to taste	
4	single boneless chicken breasts, with skin on	4
2 tbsp	butter, melted	25 mL

cream gravy

1 tbsp	all-purpose flour	15 mL
½ cup	chicken stock	125 mL
¼ cup	whipping cream	50 mL
¼ cup	grated Swiss cheese	50 mL
	Salt and freshly ground pepper to taste	

1 Preheat the oven to 375° F (190° C).
2 In a shallow dish, combine the flour, Parmesan, basil, cayenne and salt. Stir until thoroughly blended.
3 Dip the chicken into the melted butter, then into the flour mixture. Place on a buttered baking sheet and bake for 20 minutes, or until the breasts are golden and the juices run clear when the chicken is pierced.
4 To make the gravy, pour 2 tbsp (25 mL) fat from the baking sheet into a small skillet on medium-high heat. Add the flour and stir until the flour becomes straw-coloured. Pour in the chicken stock and whipping cream and bring to a boil, stirring. Stir in the cheese until it melts. Season well with salt and pepper.
5 Serve the chicken with the gravy.
Serves 4

sun-dried tomatoes

Wash, halve and seed fresh plum tomatoes. Place on racks and bake in a 175° F (80° C) oven until wrinkled and dry, 16 to 18 hours.

Sprinkle a thin layer of rock salt in the bottom of a jar. Pack in the tomatoes and cover with olive oil, making sure the tomatoes are completely immersed. Add a sprig of rosemary or a couple of dried chilies to the oil, if desired. Store in the refrigerator for one month before using.

Scatter the tomatoes into pasta sauces, chop them finely with olives for a salsa to serve with fish or mix them with cream cheese to make a spread for crackers. You can also give them away as gifts. Sun-dried tomatoes last indefinitely in the refrigerator.

chicken breasts with goat cheese

If you do not have sun-dried tomatoes, use two finely chopped fresh or canned tomatoes. Cream cheese can be substituted for the goat cheese. Linguine tossed with Pesto Butter is a perfect accompaniment.

4	**single boneless chicken breasts**	4
4 oz	**goat cheese**	**125 g**
1/3 cup	**sun-dried tomatoes, finely chopped**	**75 mL**
2 tbsp	**olive oil**	**25 mL**
1	**clove garlic, minced**	**1**
2 tbsp	**finely chopped fresh basil, or 2 tsp (10 mL) dried**	**25 mL**
pinch	**cayenne pepper**	**pinch**
	Salt and freshly ground pepper to taste	

marinade

2 tbsp	**olive oil**	**25 mL**
1 tbsp	**finely chopped fresh basil, or 1 tsp (5 mL) dried**	**15 mL**
1 tbsp	**lemon juice**	**15 mL**
1	**small clove garlic, minced**	**1**

1 Lay the chicken breasts flat and cut a slit down the long side of each breast to form a pocket.

2 In a small bowl, mix together the goat cheese, sun-dried tomatoes, 2 tbsp (25 mL) oil, 1 clove garlic, 2 tbsp (25 mL) basil and cayenne. Season with salt and pepper. Taste and adjust the seasonings.

3 Stuff the filling into the pockets in the chicken breasts. Flatten the chicken breasts with your hand to make sure the filling packs the cavity but does not overflow. Place the breasts in a flat dish.

4 In a small bowl, mix together the marinade ingredients. Pour over the chicken breasts. Marinate at room temperature for 15 minutes.

5 Remove the chicken from the marinade to a broiler pan and broil for 5 to 6 minutes on each side, or until just cooked through.

Serves 4

pesto butter

This slightly unorthodox pesto contains equal amounts of butter and oil, which give it a smooth, rich taste. Any leftovers can be frozen for use within three months. To make regular pesto, use 1/2 cup (125 mL) oil instead of 1/4 cup (50 mL) butter and 1/4 cup (50 mL) olive oil.

In a food processor or blender, chop 1 clove of garlic, 1 cup (250 mL) fresh basil leaves and 1 tbsp (15 mL) pine nuts. Process until smooth. Add 1/4 cup (50 mL) grated Parmesan cheese, 1/4 cup (50 mL) butter and 1/4 cup (50 mL) olive oil and process until smooth. Season with salt and pepper to taste.

Makes about 1 cup (250 mL)

herbed roasted chicken

If boned chicken breasts with the skin on are unavailable, use skinless breasts and drizzle with an extra tablespoon (15 mL) of olive oil. If fresh herbs are available, they will give the chicken a subtle flavour; dried herbs are more pungent. The herb combination can be changed to suit your taste. Serve with rice.

2 tsp	olive oil	10 mL
	Salt and freshly ground pepper to taste	
4	single boneless chicken breasts, with skin on	4
1	leek (dark-green leaves removed), chopped	1
1	small red pepper, chopped	1
1	small green pepper, chopped	1
4	cloves garlic, peeled	4
1/2	jalapeño pepper, seeded and chopped	1/2
1 tbsp	grated lemon rind	15 mL
1 tbsp	grated orange rind	15 mL
3	tomatoes, peeled, seeded and chopped	3
1/4 cup	chicken stock	50 mL
1 tbsp	chopped fresh rosemary, or 1 tsp (5 mL) dried	15 mL
1 tbsp	chopped fresh mint, or 1 tsp (5 mL) dried	15 mL
1 tbsp	chopped fresh tarragon, or 1 tsp (5 mL) dried	15 mL

1 Preheat the oven to 425° F (220° C).

2 Heat a large ovenproof skillet on medium heat. Add the olive oil.

3 Rub the salt and pepper into the chicken breasts. Sauté the chicken, skin side down, until the skin is browned slightly, about 2 minutes. Repeat on the second side. Remove the chicken from the skillet.

4 Add the leek, red and green peppers, garlic and jalapeño to the skillet. Sauté for 1 minute, or until the vegetables soften slightly. Add the lemon and orange rinds, tomatoes and chicken stock. Stir together and bring to a boil.

5 Place the chicken, skin side up, on top of the vegetables. Scatter with the rosemary, mint and tarragon.

6 Bake, uncovered, for 12 to 15 minutes, or until the chicken is cooked through. Serve the chicken surrounded by the sauce.
Serves 4

lemon-scented chicken

My daughter Emma loves roast chicken, and because she's always in a hurry, this recipe is perfect for her – a fast way of producing crisp-skinned, juicy roast chicken. Butterfly the bird, lay it flat and roast at a high temperature while basting frequently.

To cut the chicken into serving pieces, just cut down between the thigh and the breast to remove the leg portion and split the breast in half. The tarragon-scented sauce is slightly tart but cuts the richness of the chicken. Serve this with Garlicky Mashed Potatoes (see page 128). If you want a thicker sauce, whisk in a little arrowroot or cornstarch paste.

1	3½-lb (1.75 kg) chicken, butterflied	1
3 tbsp	chopped fresh tarragon, or 1 tbsp (15 mL) dried	45 mL
	Grated rind and juice of 1 lemon	
2 tbsp	olive oil	25 mL
	Salt and freshly ground pepper to taste	
¼ cup	balsamic or cider vinegar	50 mL
½ tsp	granulated sugar	2 mL
1 cup	chicken stock	250 mL
2 tbsp	butter	25 mL

1 Preheat the oven to 400° F (200° C).
2 Lay the chicken in a shallow roasting pan, skin side up. Sprinkle with 2 tbsp (25 mL) tarragon, the lemon rind and juice, olive oil, salt and pepper.
3 Bake for about 35 minutes, or until the juices run clear. Baste every 10 minutes.
4 Remove the chicken from the oven and place it on a carving board. Cover loosely with a tea towel.
5 In a pot, mix together the vinegar, sugar and remaining 1 tbsp (15 mL) tarragon. Bring to a boil on high heat and reduce until the liquid is syrupy. Pour in the stock and any accumulated juices from the chicken. Bring to a boil and reduce by half. Turn the heat to low and whisk in the butter.
6 Cut the chicken into 4 pieces and serve with the sauce.
Serves 4

how to butterfly a bird

Remove the wing tips. With kitchen scissors, cut through the back bone on both sides; remove the back bone. Spread the bird out as much as possible, skin side down. With scissors, cut through the V at the top of the breast bone to allow the bird to lie completely flat.

To make sure the bird roasts evenly, turn the bird skin side up and cut a slit in the breast skin beside each leg bone. Tuck the leg bones through the slits so that the legs are close to the breast. To carve the bird, cut the thighs from the breast, then split the breast in two.

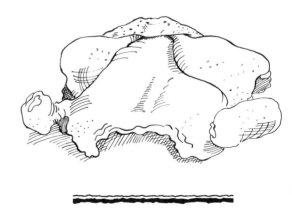

corsican chicken

A wonderfully flavoured, exciting dish that is great for buffets. This dish can be prepared a day ahead, then baked when needed. Serve with Butterfly Pasta with Basil (see page 111).

1	**head garlic**	1
6	**single boneless chicken breasts, with skin on**	6
¼ cup	**all-purpose flour**	50 mL
	Salt and freshly ground pepper to taste	
2 tbsp	**finely chopped fresh rosemary, or 2 tsp (10 mL) dried**	25 mL
3 tbsp	**olive oil**	45 mL
2 oz	**smoked ham, diced**	60 g
1	**large red onion, thickly sliced**	1
2	**tomatoes, seeded and chopped**	2
½ cup	**chopped black olives**	125 mL
3 tbsp	**brandy**	45 mL
1	**bay leaf**	1
¼ cup	**finely chopped parsley**	50 mL

1 Preheat the oven to 400° F (200° C).

2 Separate the garlic cloves and add to a small pot of water. Bring to a boil. Boil for 3 minutes, drain and peel the garlic cloves.

3 Cut each chicken breast into thirds.

4 In a shallow dish, combine the flour with salt, pepper and 1 tbsp (15 mL) rosemary. Coat the chicken pieces with the flour.

5 Heat the olive oil in a large skillet on high heat. Brown the chicken in batches, 1 to 2 minutes per side. Remove with a slotted spoon to a large ovenproof casserole.

6 Turn the heat to medium-low. Pour off all but 2 tbsp (25 mL) fat from the skillet. Add the ham, onion, garlic and remaining 1 tbsp (15 mL) rosemary.

7 Sauté until the onion is golden-brown, about 10 minutes. Add the tomatoes, olives and brandy. Bring to a boil.

8 Scrape the contents of the skillet over the chicken breasts and add the bay leaf. Cover and bake for 15 to 20 minutes, or until the chicken is cooked through. Sprinkle with the parsley before serving.

Serves 6

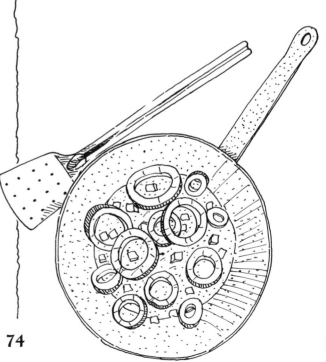

malaysian grilled chicken

In this recipe, brazil nuts are traditionally used to thicken the curry mixture, but you could substitute whole skinless almonds. You can prepare this dish up to the point of broiling, then broil when needed. If you use chicken breasts instead of legs, the simmering time will be five minutes less. Serve this dish with Warm Noodle Salad (see page 118), or with rice cooked in coconut milk instead of water.

2	cloves garlic, peeled	2
1	onion, coarsely chopped	1
1 tbsp	chopped green chili	1
1	1-inch (2.5 cm) piece fresh ginger, peeled and coarsely chopped	1
1 tsp	anchovy paste, optional	5 mL
6	Brazil nuts	6
1 cup	coconut milk	250 mL
2 tbsp	lemon juice	25 mL
	Salt and freshly ground pepper to taste	
6	chicken legs, thighs attached	6

1 In a food processor or blender, combine the garlic, onion, chili, ginger, anchovy paste and Brazil nuts. Process to a paste.
2 In a skillet large enough to hold the chicken legs in 1 layer, combine the garlic mixture with the coconut milk. Bring to a boil on high heat, turn the heat to low and simmer for 5 minutes, or until slightly thickened. Add the lemon juice.
3 Cut each chicken leg in half through the ball joint and add the pieces to the simmering sauce. Simmer, uncovered, for 30 minutes, stirring occasionally and adding some water if the sauce evaporates. Remove the chicken from the sauce.
4 Broil or barbecue the legs and thighs until browned, about 5 minutes per side, basting occasionally.
5 Reheat any remaining sauce and serve with the chicken.
Serves 6

roast cornish hens

Stuffing the birds under the skin allows the garlicky mushroom butter to seep through the flesh, making it moist and juicy. Although the recipe may look difficult, it is easy to prepare and makes a superb presentation for a special dinner or a Thanksgiving or Christmas meal. Serve with Garlicky Mashed Potatoes (see page 128) and Nutty Sprouts (see page 122).

stuffing

4 tbsp	**butter**	**60 mL**
1	**clove garlic, minced**	**1**
3	**green onions, finely chopped**	**3**
½ tsp	**dried thyme or marjoram**	**2 mL**
2 tbsp	**finely chopped parsley**	**25 mL**
½ cup	**fresh breadcrumbs**	**125 mL**
8 oz	**mushrooms, finely chopped**	**250 mL**
	Salt and freshly ground pepper to taste	
2	**Cornish hens, cut in half**	**2**

sauce

¼ cup	**wine vinegar**	**50 mL**
1 tbsp	**granulated sugar**	**15 mL**
2 cups	**chicken stock**	**500 mL**
1 tsp	**tomato paste**	**5 mL**
½ cup	**whipping cream**	**125 mL**
¼ cup	**cooked cranberries or cranberry sauce**	**50 mL**

1 Preheat the oven to 400° F (200° C).

2 To make the stuffing, in a small bowl, cream together 3 tbsp (45 mL) butter with the garlic, green onions, thyme and parsley. Beat in the breadcrumbs.

3 In a small pot over high heat, melt the remaining 1 tbsp (15 mL) butter. Add the mushrooms and sauté until there is no liquid left, 2 to 3 minutes. Blend the mushrooms into the butter/breadcrumb mixture, seasoning well with salt and pepper.

4 With your fingertips moistened with vegetable oil, gently loosen the skin around the breast of each hen by working underneath the skin. When the skin is free, continue around the thighs and legs.

5 Pack the stuffing underneath the skin around the breast, legs and thighs of each half. When finished, pat the skin all over to distribute the stuffing evenly.

6 Place the hens on a rack in a roasting pan, skin side up. Bake for 40 minutes, or until the juices run clear. (Baste the birds with the pan juices after 20 minutes.) Remove the hens from the pan to a serving platter and keep warm in a low oven.

7 To make the sauce, skim the fat from the roasting pan and add the vinegar and sugar. Place over high heat and boil until syrupy. Add the stock and tomato paste and reduce the liquid by half. Swirl in the cream and continue cooking until slightly thickened. Scatter in the cranberries. Pour the sauce over the hens before serving.

Serves 4

chicken with garlic and lemon

The lemony sauce and the soft mellow garlic cloves make a tantalizing dish for that special dinner or buffet. In my classes this is often voted the best recipe we make. If you wish to use boneless chicken breasts, they will cook in about 15 minutes in the sauce.

2	lemons	2
1	head garlic	1
3 cups	chicken stock	750 mL
4	single chicken breasts	4
	Salt and freshly ground pepper to taste	
1 tsp	dried thyme	5 mL
2 tbsp	olive oil	25 mL
3 tbsp	all-purpose flour	45 mL
¼ cup	dry white wine	50 mL

1 Grate the rind from the lemons and reserve. Remove any remaining peel and white pith from the lemons and cut the flesh into thin slices.

2 Separate the garlic cloves and combine with the stock in a small pot. Bring to a boil over medium heat and simmer for 3 minutes. Strain the stock and reserve. Cool the garlic cloves slightly, then slip the skins off.

3 Preheat the oven to 375° F (190° C).

4 Sprinkle the chicken with salt, pepper and thyme.

5 Heat the oil in a large skillet over medium-high heat. Cook the breasts, skin side down, for 5 minutes per side, or until golden-brown. Transfer the chicken to an ovenproof dish and discard all but 3 tbsp (45 mL) fat from the skillet.

6 Stir the flour into the skillet and cook, stirring, until straw-coloured, about 2 minutes. Add the wine, reserved stock and grated rind. Bring to a boil, stirring.

7 Top the chicken with the garlic, lemon slices and wine/stock sauce. Cover and bake for 25 to 30 minutes, or until the chicken is just tender. If the sauce is not thick enough, pour it into a skillet and reduce over medium heat until it coats a spoon. Pour back over the chicken.

Serves 4

cooking garlic

When whole garlic is cooked for a long time, it loses its characteristic bite and becomes a mellow, mild-mannered vegetable. To avoid having to peel individual cloves, hold the whole garlic head by the stem end and cut through the root to expose the ends of the cloves. Separate the cloves and toss into a small pot of water. Bring to a boil and cook for 3 minutes. Drain well. You should be able to squeeze the cloves right out of their skins.

chicken livers with paprika and sour cream

This slightly spicy dish should be served with noodles or rice to absorb the sauce.

2 tbsp	vegetable oil	25 mL
1 lb	chicken livers	500 mL
	Salt and freshly	
	ground pepper to taste	
1	onion, diced	1
1	green pepper, diced	1
½ cup	chopped tomato	125 mL
½ cup	chicken stock	125 mL
1 tbsp	paprika	15 mL
½ cup	sour cream	125 mL
2 tbsp	chopped fresh dill	25 mL

1 In a large skillet, heat the oil on high heat. Add the chicken livers and sauté, stirring frequently, until golden-brown, about 3 minutes. Remove from the skillet and season with salt and pepper.

2 Add the onion and green pepper to the skillet and sauté until softened, about 2 minutes.

3 Stir in the tomato, chicken stock and paprika. Bring to a boil, reduce heat to medium, cover and simmer for 5 minutes. Stir in the sour cream and chicken livers.

4 Reheat but do not bring to the boil. Season well with salt and pepper and sprinkle with dill before serving.

Serves 4

crispy roast duck with crunchy potatoes

Some people complain that they don't like to eat duck because of its high fat content and the difficulty with carving. I have developed this method that will produce crisp duck with less fat and no carving problems. The duck is cut up into pieces and the legs go into the oven first because they take longer to cook than breasts.

To make the potatoes really crunchy, they first simmer in the water under the duck and, as the water evaporates, they cook in the duck fat and become a crunchy golden mass.

1	4- to 5-lb (2 to 2.5 kg) duck,	1
	cut into 4 pieces	
1	clove garlic, sliced	1
2 tbsp	soy sauce	25 mL
3	potatoes, peeled	3

½ cup	water	125 mL
1 tsp	dried sage	5 mL
	Salt and freshly	
	ground pepper to taste	

1 Preheat the oven to 450°F (230° C).

2 Insert 2 garlic slices under the skin of each duck quarter. Rub the top of the duck skin with soy sauce.

3 Cut the potatoes into 1-inch (2.5 cm) cubes and place in the bottom of a roasting pan. Pour in the water and sprinkle with the sage, salt and pepper.

4 Place the duck legs on a rack over the potatoes. Roast for 10 minutes. Reduce the heat to 400° F (200° C) and place the breasts on the rack. Roast for a further 30 minutes.

5 Place the duck on a serving plate and arrange the potatoes around the duck.

Serves 4

If you buy a frozen duck, defrost it for 24 hours in the refrigerator. With a heavy chef's knife or cleaver, remove the wing tips. Slice through the breast bone, then with kitchen scissors cut through on both sides of the back bone. This should give you two half ducks and one back bone. Discard the back bone or save for making duck stock.

Slice between the leg and breast on each side. You will have four pieces. Trim away any fat, especially under the skin.

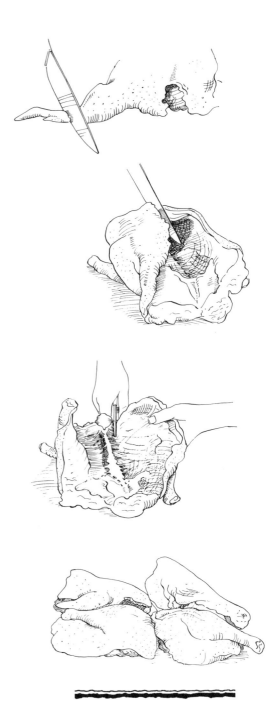

chicken and rice casserole

A quick one-dish meal with lots of flavour. Substitute chicken breasts for the legs if desired.

2 tbsp	vegetable oil	25 mL
4	chicken legs, thighs attached	4
1/4 tsp	salt	1 mL
1/4 tsp	freshly ground pepper	1 mL
2	leeks (dark-green leaves removed), chopped, or 1 onion, chopped	2
1	clove garlic, finely chopped	1
1 cup	diced green peppers	250 mL
1 cup	diced red peppers	250 mL
1 tsp	dried oregano	5 mL
1 tsp	dried basil	5 mL
2 tbsp	finely chopped parsley	25 mL
pinch	cayenne pepper	pinch
2 cups	chicken stock	500 mL
	Juice of 1 lemon	
1 cup	long-grain rice	250 mL

1 Heat the oil in a large skillet on medium heat. Season the chicken with salt and pepper.

2 Cook the chicken legs for about 5 minutes per side, or until golden-brown. Remove from the skillet.

3 Add the leeks, garlic and peppers to the skillet and sauté until softened, about 3 minutes.

4 Stir in the oregano, basil, parsley and cayenne. Pour in the stock and lemon juice. Bring to a boil and add the rice.

5 Reduce the heat to low; return the chicken to pan. Cover and simmer for 30 minutes, or until the rice is cooked and juices run clear.

Serves 4

quick tips for leftover chicken

- **Chicken Sandwich:** Spread mayonnaise on one slice of bread and chutney or cranberry sauce on the other. Top with slices of cooked chicken, alfalfa sprouts and lettuce and sandwich together.
- **Chicken Schnitzel:** Dredge slices of cooked chicken in flour seasoned with salt and pepper and quickly sauté in butter until browned. Serve topped with sour cream.
- **Devilled Chicken Joints:** Spread leftover cooked wings or legs with Dijon mustard mixed with Worcestershire sauce and minced garlic. Broil until golden-brown. Serve hot or cold.
- **Quick Chicken Salad:** Combine chopped cooked chicken with mayonnaise, chopped green onion, chopped cucumber and a pinch of curry powder. Stuff into a pita.

chapter six

BEEF, LAMB, PORK & VEAL

*R*emember when families traditionally sat down to a large roast for Sunday dinner? Today this custom has almost disappeared because of the fat content, price and time it takes to cook a large piece of meat. However, meat adapts beautifully to fast cooking when you use tender cuts and grill or sauté them.

BEEF

Many people regard steak as the ultimate fast food, but recently it has lost some of its appeal because of its high cholesterol content. In fact, the leaner cuts of beef are ideal for fast cooking, and they lend themselves to a variety of interesting dishes.

tips

■ For the cook in a hurry, only certain cuts of beef work successfully. Use cuts such as filet for quick roasting (although it is expensive, there is hardly any fat and no waste).

■ For grilling or frying, use porterhouse, T-bone, rib steaks, flank steaks or sirloin.

■ The less expensive, leaner flank steak or boneless sirloin are best for stir-fries or for grilled steaks served rare.

■ Look for beef that is dark red, firm to the touch and with white fat. When beef is exposed to the air, it turns brownish-red. This is the sign of aging – a process that improves flavour and tenderness.

■ Store beef loosely wrapped in waxed paper in the meat drawer of the refrigerator for up to three days. Ground beef should be used within two days.

mexican hamburgers

The chili cheese butter turns a plain hamburger into a special and trendy new dish. (The butter should keep, refrigerated, for up to one week.) Serve the burgers wrapped in a flour tortilla for extra authenticity.

To prevent hamburgers from falling apart on the grill, try to combine all the ingredients very gently.

2 lb	lean ground beef	1 kg
1	small onion, chopped	1
¼ cup	sour cream	50 mL
1 tbsp	chili powder	15 mL
½ tsp	salt	2 mL

chili cheese butter

½ cup	butter, at room temperature	125 mL
¼ cup	grated Cheddar cheese	50 mL
1 tsp	chili powder	5 mL
¼ tsp	dried chili flakes	1 mL
	Salt and freshly ground pepper to taste	

1 In a large bowl, gently combine the beef, onion, sour cream, 1 tbsp (15 mL) chili powder and salt.

2 Shape the meat into 6 patties ½ inch (1.25 cm) thick.

3 Barbecue or broil the hamburgers for 4 minutes per side for medium-rare.

4 Meanwhile, in a small bowl, cream together all the ingredients for the butter.
5 Top each hamburger with 1 tbsp (15 mL) butter before serving.

Serves 6

light-style meatloaf

An easy meatloaf with lots of flavour, texture and fibre but with a low fat content. It's a standby in our house. By mixing beef and turkey together, you reduce the fat while retaining flavour. If turkey is unavailable, use ground veal.

½ cup	rolled oats	125 mL
3 tbsp	skim milk	45 mL
12 oz	ground turkey	375 g
12 oz	lean ground beef	375 g
½ cup	shredded carrot	125 mL
1	small onion, chopped	1
½ tsp	dried thyme	2 mL
½ tsp	dried marjoram	2 mL
1	egg	1
½ tsp	salt	2 mL
½ tsp	freshly ground pepper	2 mL

sauce

1 tbsp	ketchup	15 mL
1 tsp	Worcestershire sauce	5 mL
1 tbsp	soy sauce	15 mL
¼ tsp	Tabasco	1 mL

1 Preheat the oven to 350° F (180° C).
2 In a large bowl, combine all the ingredients except the sauce ingredients. Spoon into a 9 x 5-inch (2 L) loaf pan. Bake for 30 minutes.
3 Meanwhile, combine the ketchup, Worcestershire, soy sauce and Tabasco. Make three slits on top of the meatloaf. Brush with the sauce, making sure some sauces gets into the slits.
4 Bake for another 30 minutes, or until the juices run clear. Pour off any fat that accumulates in the pan. Unmould onto a carving board and let sit for 5 minutes before slicing.

Serves 6

oatmeal

Oatmeal is rich in B vitamins and has lots of fibre. It is marketed in three different forms – rolled oats (regular oatmeal), quick-cooking oatmeal and instant oatmeal. Rolled oats are thick cut and take longer to cook than the other types. This form of oatmeal is the most nutritious and tasty. Quick-cooking oatmeal is rolled finer but loses something in nutrition, flavour and texture. Instant oatmeal is rather like baby food – it's a thick and gummy breakfast cereal.

aromatic beef with pinot noir sauce

To roast fillet accurately, measure the meat vertically at its thickest part. Roast 12 minutes per 1 inch (2.5 cm) at 425 F (210 C) for rare, 15 minutes for medium rare and 20 minutes for medium.

1	3-lb (1.50 kg) fillet of beef	1
1/3 cup	chopped Italian parsley	75 mL
1 tbsp	chopped chives	15 mL
1/2 tsp	chopped fresh mint	2 mL
2 tsp	chopped fresh basil	10 mL
1/4 tsp	dried rosemary	1 mL
2	cloves garlic, minced	2
2 tbsp	gin	25 mL
1/4 tsp	ground allspice	1 mL
1 tbsp	oil	15 mL
3 tbsp	butter	45 mL
2 cups	pinot noir wine	500 mL
4 cups	beef stock	1 L

1 Trim beef fillet of fat and any sinew. Tie meat at half-inch (1 cm) intervals for even roasting.

2 Mix together herbs, garlic, gin, allspice and oil. Blend 1 tbsp herb mixture into butter, cover and reserve in refrigerator. Rub remaining herb mixture onto beef. Refrigerate beef for 48 hours.

3 To make sauce, reduce wine in a medium pot until only 1/4 cup (50 mL) remains. Add stock and reduce until mixture lightly coats a spoon.

4 Preheat oven to 425 F (210 C) and roast fillet for 15 minutes per 1 inch (2.5 cm) for medium rare. Remove from oven and let stand for 10 minutes.

5 Reheat sauce on low heat. Whisk in reserved herb butter.

6 Slice meat into thin slices and serve with sauce.

Serves 6

peppercorns

Peppercorns come in many colours. Black peppercorns are picked unripe and dried to give us the familiar wrinkled skin. White peppercorns are ripe ones that have had the outer black shells removed. (Black pepper is stronger than white pepper.) Green peppercorns are picked unripe and are preserved in vinegar or brine. They have a mild taste with a slight tang.

Always use freshly ground peppercorns, because they have a full, fragrant, spicy taste that disappears quickly after grinding. Preground pepper has already lost most of its flavour.

beef niçoise

This is one of the best summer entertaining dishes I know. It takes no time to make, it can be served hot or cold. Serve it with Eggplant Tomato Salad (see page 145).

1	4-lb (2 kg) beef tenderloin	1
1 tbsp	coarse-grained mustard	15 mL
1 tbsp	Dijon mustard	15 mL
1 tbsp	soy sauce	15 mL
1	clove garlic, minced	1
½ tsp	cayenne pepper	2 mL

niçoise sauce

2	cloves garlic, peeled	2
1	egg yolk	1
2 tbsp	dry red wine	25 mL
½ cup	olive oil	125 mL
4	anchovies, finely chopped	4
2 tbsp	finely chopped parsley	25 mL
2 tbsp	finely chopped chives	25 mL
	Juice of 1 lime	
	Freshly ground pepper to taste	

1 Trim the beef of all fat.

2 In a small bowl, combine the mustards, soy sauce, minced garlic and cayenne. Coat the beef evenly on all sides and marinate for 30 minutes at room temperature.

3 Preheat the oven to 425° F (220° C).

4 Place the meat on a rack in a roasting pan and bake for 30 to 35 minutes, or until pink juices begin to rise to the surface. Remove to a platter and cool.

5 Meanwhile, in a food processor or blender, with the machine running, drop 2 cloves garlic through the feed tube and chop finely. Add the egg yolk and red wine and blend. With the machine running, slowly add the olive oil through the feed tube. Fold in the anchovies, parsley, chives and lime juice. Season with pepper.

6 Cut the meat into thin slices and overlap on a platter. Serve the sauce on the side.

Serves 10 to 12

To cook beef tenderloin properly, consider its thickness instead of its weight. Measure the meat vertically at its thickest point, then allow 12 minutes per 1 inch (2.5 cm) roasting time for rare and 15 minutes for medium.

stilton butter

A good butter to serve with beef. You can also use Roquefort or Danish blue cheese.

In a bowl, beat together ½ cup (125 mL) softened butter with ¼ cup (50 mL) crumbled Stilton cheese, 2 tbsp (25 mL) finely chopped parsley, 2 tbsp (25 mL) finely chopped chives, 1 tbsp (15 mL) lemon juice and freshly ground pepper to taste. Chill.

Makes about ¾ cup (175 mL)

savoury mince

An old Scottish meal-in-one-dish that I remember eating every week as a child. Mince is the Scottish word for ground beef. This dish has to be highly seasoned – most good Scots would throw in some HP sauce as a final flavouring. Serve it with a green salad. This dish reheats well.

2 tbsp	vegetable oil	25 mL
1	onion, thinly sliced	1
1	clove garlic, finely chopped	1
1 lb	lean ground beef	500 g
1 tbsp	Dijon mustard	15 mL
pinch	cayenne pepper	pinch
2 cups	chopped tomato	500 mL
1	bay leaf	1
	Salt and freshly ground pepper to taste	
1 tsp	Worcestershire sauce	5 mL
4	potatoes, peeled and diced	4
4 oz	mushrooms, chopped	125 g
½	green pepper, chopped	½

1 In a skillet on high heat, heat the oil. Stir in the onion and sauté until softened slightly, about 2 minutes.
2 Lower the heat to medium and add the garlic and beef. Sauté until the meat loses its pinkness. Stir in the mustard and cayenne.
3 Add the tomato, bay leaf, salt, pepper, Worcestershire sauce and potatoes. Bring the mixture to a boil, cover and simmer for 30 minutes.

4 Stir in the mushrooms and green pepper. Cook, covered, for another 15 minutes, or until the potatoes are tender. Taste for seasoning, adding salt, pepper or HP sauce, if needed.
Serves 4

beef fajitas with mango salsa

The fajitas can be made ahead and served prewrapped at room temperature, but I like them best with the tortillas warm from the barbecue or oven and the steak juicy and hot. If fresh mint is unavailable for the salsa, use 1 tbsp (15 mL) mint sauce. Or, instead of making the mango salsa, buy a spicy commercial salsa.

1 lb	flank steak	500 g

marinade

3 tbsp	lemon juice	45 mL
2	cloves garlic, minced	2
1	small onion, finely chopped	1
1 tbsp	chili powder	15 mL
1 tsp	ground cumin	5 mL
1 tsp	liquid honey	5 mL
1 tbsp	vegetable oil	15 mL
½ tsp	salt	2 mL

mango salsa

1	medium mango, peeled and chopped	1
1 tsp	finely chopped jalapeño pepper, or to taste	5 mL
3	green onions, chopped	3
3 tbsp	finely chopped green pepper	45 mL
	Grated rind and juice of 1 lime	
2 tbsp	chopped fresh mint	25 mL
1 tbsp	mango chutney	15 mL
	Salt to taste	
12	flour tortillas	12

1 Score the flank steak on the surface of one side to prevent curling.

2 In a large baking dish, combine the marinade ingredients. Add the steak and coat with marinade on both sides. Marinate for 30 minutes at room temperature.

3 In a medium bowl, combine the ingredients for the salsa. Cover and refrigerate until needed.

4 Broil or barbecue the steak for 3 to 4 minutes per side for rare. Remove to a carving board and slice into very thin slices against the grain.

5 Warm the tortillas in the oven or on the barbecue.

6 In each tortilla, place 3 overlapping slices of meat and top with 1 tbsp (15 mL) salsa. Roll up the tortilla around the meat and cut each roll in half. Serve warm or cold. Alternatively, place the meat, tortillas and a bowl of salsa on a platter and let guests assemble their own fajitas.

Serves 6

tortillas

Tortillas are pancake-like breads originating in Mexico. There are two kinds – corn and flour. Corn tortillas are the basis of many Mexican foods. They are made into tacos (stuffed fried corn tortillas), enchiladas (stuffed baked tortillas rather like a Mexican crêpe) or tostadas (flat golden-brown fried tortillas topped with various combinations of salads, meats and fish).

Flour tortillas are made into quesadillas, a pizza-like dish topped with salsa, cheese, chilies and meats. They can also be used to wrap any kind of filling to be eaten with the fingers.

87

LAMB

Mild, tender lamb is gaining popularity in Canada. Its lack of fat, tender texture, delicate taste and the speed with which it can be cooked make it a good choice.

tips

- Boneless butterflied lamb legs, spread flat, broil or bake quickly. Tender rib and loin chops can be fried or grilled.
- Flavour lamb with rosemary, mustard, soy sauce, garlic, lemon and lime. East Indian spices such as cumin and coriander bring out the sweetness in lamb.
- When buying lamb, make sure the flesh is rosy pink and the fat is white.
- If you can't buy fresh Canadian lamb, frozen lamb is an acceptable substitute. Frozen New Zealand lamb is tender, flavourful and less expensive than domestic lamb. To defrost it, leave it in its packaging and place in the refrigerator for 24 hours. The slow defrosting will give you much moister meat because less juice will leak out.
- Lamb should be served pink for the best flavour and texture.

rack of lamb provençale with garlic confit

Garlic loses all its strong flavours and becomes a mellow vegetable when it is cooked. Its flavour beautifully complements the lamb.

garlic confit

1	head garlic	1
2 tbsp	butter	25 mL

lamb

2	lamb racks, 8 chops each	2
1 tbsp	Dijon mustard	15 mL
1 tbsp each	chopped fresh rosemary and thyme or 1 tsp (5 mL) dried	15 mL
2 tbsp	chopped parsley	25 mL
1/2 cup	fresh breadcrumbs	125 mL
2 tbsp	olive oil	25 mL
	Salt and freshly ground pepper to taste	

sauce

1/2 cup	red wine	125 mL
1 tbsp	sherry or apple cider vinegar	15 mL
1/4 tsp	sugar	1 mL
1 cup	chicken stock	250 mL
1/4 cup	unsalted butter	50 mL
1 tbsp	chopped parsley	15 mL

1 To make garlic confit, separate garlic head into cloves. Slice root end off each clove but do not peel. Place in small pot,

88

cover with water and boil 5 minutes. Drain and slip garlic out of its skin. Heat butter in skillet on low heat, add garlic cloves, cover and cook, shaking pan occasionally, until garlic is golden, about 10 minutes. Reserve garlic and skillet for sauce.

2 Cut away last 2 inches (5 cm) of fat and meat from bones. Trim remaining fat. Cut racks in half. In a small bowl, combine mustard, rosemary, thyme, parsley, breadcrumbs, oil, salt and pepper. Pat over lamb racks.

3 Preheat oven to 400 F (200 C). Place lamb on a rack over roasting pan and bake for 35 to 45 minutes, or until juices are slightly pink. Let stand for 10 minutes before carving.

4 To make sauce, combine red wine, vinegar and sugar in reserved skillet. Boil until liquid is reduced to a glaze, about 3 minutes. Add stock and butter and boil until slightly thickened. Scatter in garlic cloves and parsley.

5 To serve, slice lamb into chops, spoon on some sauce and one or two garlic cloves.

Serves 4

new zealand hamburgers

Ground lamb has a delicate flavour and texture and is a change from beef. Excellent lamb comes from New Zealand, as does this recipe from Annabelle Langbein, a wonderful New Zealand cook. Serve the burgers on crusty egg bread and top with Mint Mayonnaise and a piece of kiwi.

1 lb	ground lamb	500 g
1 tbsp	ketchup	15 mL
	Salt and freshly ground pepper to taste	
1 tsp	dried basil	5 mL
2	green onions, finely chopped	2
1 tbsp	finely chopped parsley	15 mL
1 tbsp	vegetable oil	15 mL

1 In a large bowl, combine the lamb, ketchup, salt, pepper, basil, onions and parsley. Form into 3 patties. Brush with the oil.

2 Place the burgers on a rack over a roasting pan. Grill for 4 minutes per side, or until the juices rise to the surface of the meat.

Serves 3

mint mayonnaise

In a bowl, combine ½ cup (125 mL) mayonnaise with 1 tbsp (15 mL) mint sauce. Season with freshly ground pepper. Garnish with a sprig of fresh mint.

Makes ½ cup (125 mL)

stir-fried lamb and garlic

The best lamb to use for this stir-fry is boneless loin, available at some supermarkets in the frozen food section. Or, have the butcher cut you a lamb steak from a roast, or buy three lamb chops. Serve with Indonesian Fried Rice (see page 108).

8 oz	boneless lamb	250 g

marinade

1 tbsp	wine vinegar	15 mL
1 tbsp	soy sauce	15 mL
1 tbsp	vegetable oil	15 mL
1 tsp	granulated sugar	5 mL
6	green onions	6
3	cloves garlic	3

sauce

1 tbsp	soy sauce	15 mL
1 tbsp	rice vinegar	15 mL
½ tsp	Chinese chili sauce	2 mL
1 tsp	sesame oil	5 mL
2 tbsp	vegetable oil	25 mL

1 Slice the lamb into thin strips across the grain. Set aside.

2 To make the marinade, in a medium bowl, combine the wine vinegar, 1 tbsp (15 mL) soy sauce, 1 tbsp (15 mL) oil and sugar. Add the lamb slices and marinate at room temperature for 15 minutes.

3 Slice the onions in half lengthwise, then slice diagonally into 2-inch (5 cm) strips. Thinly slice the garlic. Set both aside.

4 To make the sauce, in a small bowl, combine 1 tbsp (15 mL) soy sauce with the rice vinegar, chili sauce and sesame oil.

5 On high heat, heat a wok or large skillet until very hot. Add 2 tbsp (25 mL) oil. Add the lamb in 2 batches and stir-fry until browned. Remove from the wok and reserve. Add the garlic and onions and stir-fry until wilted, about 1 minute.

6 Return the lamb to the wok, pour in the sauce and stir everything together. Bring to a boil. Serve immediately.

Serves 2

mint sauce

This homemade mint sauce can be served with any grilled or roasted lamb.

Add 2 cups (500 mL) mint leaves and 2 tbsp (25 mL) granulated sugar to the bowl of a food processor. Process until the mint is finely chopped. Add ¼ cup (50 mL) hot water and combine again to dissolve the sugar. Scrape into a bowl and add about ½ cup (125 mL) vinegar, or to taste. The sauce should keep for at least three weeks.

Makes 1 cup (250 mL)

PORK

Pork is sometimes known as the "other white meat" because it has a lower cholesterol count than beef. Pork is also relatively inexpensive. It has a rich, subtle flavour but isn't too heavy. It can be used in speedy stir-fries and can be braised in under an hour.

tips

■ Mildly flavoured pork tenderloin cooks quickly and can be used in stir-fries or roasts.

■ Pork chops are a quick and inexpensive staple in most homes. They can be fried, baked, grilled or braised.

■ Pork goes well with rosemary, apples, sage, thyme, prunes and cabbage.

■ Today it is considered quite safe to cook pork slightly pink for the best flavour and texture.

■ Look for a pearly pink-coloured flesh with firm white fat. Avoid cuts that are dark pink or have yellowish fat. Fresh pork has no smell.

■ Store pork loosely wrapped in waxed paper in the refrigerator up to two days.

barbecued pork

A fast way to produce a flavourful Chinese roast pork.

1	1½-lb (750 g) pork tenderloin	1

marinade

3 tbsp	soy sauce	45 mL
2 tbsp	dry white wine	25 mL
1 tbsp	grated fresh ginger	15 mL
¼ cup	hoisin sauce	50 mL
2 tbsp	liquid honey	25 mL
1 tbsp	sesame oil	15 mL

1 Divide the pork into 4-inch (10 cm) sections.

2 In a large bowl, combine the marinade ingredients and add the pork. Turn the pork until evenly coated; then marinate for 30 minutes at room temperature, turning at least once.

3 Preheat the oven to 450° F (230° C).

4 Remove the pork from the marinade; reserve the marinade. Place the pork on a rack over a foil-covered baking sheet. Roast for 15 minutes. Lower the heat to 375° F (190° C), brush the meat with more marinade and roast for another 15 to 20 minutes, or until the juices run clear.

5 In a small pot over high heat, bring the remaining marinade to a boil and cook until it thickens, 2 to 5 minutes. Brush over the pork and let cool.

Serves 4

pork chops with vermouth and lemon

This dish also works well with veal chops. If you don't have dry vermouth, substitute white wine.

4	shoulder or rib pork chops, about 1 inch (2.5 cm) thick	4
	Salt and freshly ground pepper to taste	
2 tbsp	all-purpose flour	25 mL
¼ cup	butter	50 mL
½ cup	dry vermouth	125 mL
	Grated rind and juice of ½ lemon	
½ cup	whipping cream	125 mL
2 tbsp	finely chopped parsley	25 mL

1 Season the chops with salt and pepper, then coat in flour.

2 In a large skillet, heat the butter on medium heat until it sizzles. Add the chops and slowly brown on both sides, about 3 minutes per side. Reduce the heat to low and cover the pan. Simmer slowly, turning the chops occasionally, for 30 to 45 minutes, or until the chops are fork-tender.

3 Remove the chops from the pan. Over high heat, add the vermouth and stir up any bits that are left at the bottom of the pan.

4 Boil to reduce the liquid by half, about 1 minute. Add the lemon rind and juice and boil the mixture for 1 minute longer. Pour in the cream and reduce the sauce until slightly thickened, about 1 minute. Sprinkle in the parsley and pour the sauce over the chops.

Serves 4

sausages with onion sauce

A fast supper served with Sautéed Potatoes with Rosemary (see page 130) or Bacon Cheddar Muffins (see page 156) or Cabbage with Grainy Mustard (see page 125).

1½ lb	bratwurst sausages	750 g
2	large onions, sliced	2
2 tbsp	butter	25 mL
2 tbsp	all-purpose flour	25 mL
1 cup	beef stock	250 mL
1 tbsp	Dijon mustard	15 mL
1 tbsp	tomato paste	15 mL
	Salt and freshly ground pepper to taste	

1 Barely cover the bottom of a large skillet with hot water. Add the sausages, cover and simmer on medium heat until the water has evaporated and the sausages are cooked, about 15 minutes.

2 Uncover and continue to brown the sausages, turning in the fat released into the pan. When they are brown, remove and cut into thick slices. Reserve.

3 Add the onions to the skillet and sauté until the onions are golden and soft, about 5 minutes. Remove from the skillet and reserve.

4 Pour off any fat and add the butter to the skillet. Stir in the flour and continue to stir frequently until the flour is straw-coloured, about 3 minutes.

5 Stir in the stock, mustard and tomato paste. Bring to a boil, stirring. Add salt and pepper and return the sausages to the skillet. Simmer together for 5 minutes, or until the sausages are hot.

Serves 4

stir-fried pork with garlic chili sauce

A tangy Chinese stir-fry that tastes great with steamed rice and broccoli. If Chinese chili sauce is unavailable, use ½ tsp (2 mL) Tabasco.

8 oz	boneless pork	250 g
1 tbsp	soy sauce	15 mL
4 tsp	cornstarch	20 mL
1 tbsp	water	15 mL
1 tsp	Chinese chili sauce	5 mL
1 tbsp	vinegar	15 mL
¼ cup	chicken stock	50 mL
1 tsp	sesame oil	5 mL
2 tbsp	vegetable oil	25 mL
4	cloves garlic, finely chopped	4
1 tbsp	finely chopped fresh ginger	15 mL
2 tbsp	finely chopped green onion	25 mL

1 Slice the pork into slivers across the grain.

2 In a medium bowl, mix together the soy sauce, 3 tsp (15 mL) cornstarch and water. Stir in the pork and marinate at room temperature for 15 minutes.

3 In a small bowl, combine the chili sauce, remaining 1 tsp (5 mL) cornstarch, vinegar, chicken stock and sesame oil. Reserve.

4 In wok or large skillet, heat the oil on high heat. Add the garlic and ginger. Stir-fry until fragrant, about 1 minute. Add the pork and stir-fry for 1 minute.

5 Add the rest of the marinade and the chili sauce mixture to the skillet. Mix together and bring to a boil; cook for 1 minute longer, stirring constantly, until the sauce thickens. Garnish with chopped green onion.

Serves 2 or 3

pork tenderloin with apples and brandy

Serve with thyme-scented roast potatoes and green beans garnished with diced red pepper.

1 tbsp	olive oil	15 mL
1 lb	pork tenderloin	500 g
Salt and freshly ground pepper to taste		
1 tbsp	chopped fresh rosemary	15 mL
1 cup	apple juice or cider	250 mL
2 tbsp	liquid honey	25 mL
1 tbsp	Dijon mustard	15 mL
2	cloves garlic, chopped	2
1/4 tsp	black pepper	1 mL
3	apples, peeled, cored and sliced into wedges	3
2 tbsp	lemon juice	25 mL
2 tbsp	butter	25 mL
1/2 cup	whipping cream	125 mL
1/4 cup	brandy	50 mL
1 tbsp	balsamic vinegar	15 mL
1 tbsp	chopped parsley	15 mL

1 Preheat oven to 350 F (180 C).

2 Heat olive oil in skillet on medium-high heat. Cut tenderloin in half to fit skillet. Season with salt, pepper and rosemary. Add to skillet and brown on all sides, about 3 minutes. Remove tenderloin to baking dish and drain fat from skillet.

3 Add apple juice, 1 tbsp (15 mL) honey, mustard and garlic to skillet. Whisk and bring to boil. Pour sauce over tenderloin. Cover and bake for 20 to 30 minutes, or until pork is no longer pink.

4 Meanwhile, toss apples with lemon juice. Melt butter in a skillet over medium-high heat. Add apples, drizzle with remaining 1 tbsp (15 mL) honey and sauté until apples are softened and glazed. Reserve. Apples can be served warm or cold.

5 When meat is cooked, remove to a serving dish and keep warm. Pour sauce into skillet. Add cream and brandy and bring to boil. Boil 4 to 5 minutes, or until sauce has thickened. Stir in balsamic vinegar and parsley.

6 Slice tenderloin into 1/2-inch (1.25 cm) thick slices. Drizzle with sauce and serve apples on the side.

Serves 4

cooking apples

Use tart apples in savoury sauces or soups. My favourites are Granny Smiths (a tart green apple that does not grow in Canada because it needs a longer growing season), Spys (the best Canadian cooking apple, also delicious for eating) or Mutsus (a cross between a Golden Delicious and a crisp Japanese variety).

VEAL

Veal is a boon to the person in a hurry because it is tender, needs no preparation and can be cooked in an instant. Although the most tender cuts are expensive, there is very little fat or waste.

tips

■ Veal scaloppine is one of the fastest dishes you can cook, and it adapts to many different flavours. Try cooking it with sage, tarragon, rosemary, lemon, orange, cream or tomatoes.

■ Look for pale, creamy-coloured veal. Provimi veal is the finest you can buy.

■ Veal loses its texture and taste when it is frozen. To store it, take it out of its plastic wrap and wrap it loosely in waxed paper. Ground veal must be used within a day; other cuts should be used within two days.

■ Tougher cuts like shoulder chops can be braised in under an hour.

■ Veal loses its juices more quickly than other meats. Do not overcook it, or the meat will dry out.

hungarian veal burgers

Serve this on rye bread with sour dill pickles and extra sour cream.

1 tbsp	vegetable oil	15 mL
½	green pepper, finely chopped	½
1	small onion, finely chopped	1
1 lb	ground veal	500 g
2 tbsp	sour cream	25 mL
1 tsp	paprika	5 mL
2 tbsp	finely chopped fresh dill	25 mL
	Salt and freshly ground pepper to taste	
1 tbsp	vegetable oil	15 mL

1 Heat the oil in a large skillet on high heat. Sauté the green pepper and onion until softened, about 2 minutes.

2 In a medium bowl, combine the pepper and onion with the veal. Blend in the sour cream, paprika and dill. Season well with salt and pepper and divide into 3 patties.

3 Brush the patties with oil and grill for 4 minutes per side.

Serves 3

veal chili with black beans

A modern chili using canned black beans and stewing veal. This dish is lighter than the regular beef chili and is good on a buffet served with cornbread or biscuits and a salad. If you can't find canned black or turtle beans, use white or red kidney beans.

The preparation is very quick, although the chili does take about an hour to cook.

2 tbsp	vegetable oil	25 mL
2 lb	veal stewing meat, cut into	1 kg
	1-inch (2.5 cm) cubes	
	Salt and freshly	
	ground pepper to taste	
1	large onion, chopped	1
4	cloves garlic, finely chopped	4
3 tbsp	chili powder	45 mL
1 tbsp	ground cumin	15 mL
1 tbsp	ground coriander	15 mL
1 tsp	dried oregano	5 mL
¼ tsp	cayenne pepper	1 mL
3 cups	beef stock	750 mL
2 tsp	grated orange rind	10 mL
2 cups	cooked or canned black beans	500 mL
	Sour cream	
	Grated orange rind	
	Chopped fresh coriander	

1 In a large pot, heat the oil on high heat. Add the veal (in batches if necessary) and brown on all sides. Remove the meat from the pan and season with salt and pepper.

2 Lower the heat to medium and add the onion. Cook, stirring frequently, for 3 minutes, or until softened. Add the garlic and cook for 30 seconds.

3 Return the meat to the pot and stir together with the onions and garlic. Stir in the chili powder, cumin, coriander, oregano and cayenne. Cook, stirring, for 1 minute, or until you can smell the spices.

4 Add the beef stock and orange rind. Bring to a boil, stirring occasionally. Reduce the heat to medium-low and simmer, covered, for 40 minutes.

5 Add the beans and simmer, uncovered, for 20 minutes more, or until the meat is tender. Season with salt and pepper. Serve each portion garnished with sour cream, a sprinkle of orange rind and coriander.

Serves 6

braised veal chops with leeks and orange

Shoulder veal chops are an inexpensive, tasty cut. Serve them with linguine noodles and green beans. Substitute veal stewing meat or pork chops, if desired.

4	**veal shoulder chops, about ½ inch**	4
	(1.25 cm) thick	
2 tsp	**dried basil**	10 mL
	Juice of 1 orange	
1 cup	**all-purpose flour**	250 mL
	Salt and freshly	
	ground pepper to taste	
2 tbsp	**vegetable oil**	25 mL
3	**leeks (dark-green leaves removed),**	3
	sliced	
4	**cloves garlic, finely chopped**	4
1	**4-inch (10 cm) piece orange rind**	1
¼ cup	**tomato sauce**	50 mL
2 cups	**chicken stock**	500 mL
2 tbsp	**chopped fresh dill**	25 mL

1 Preheat the oven to 350° F (180° C). Remove any excess fat from the chops.

2 In a small bowl or cup, combine the basil and the orange juice. Pour over chops.

3 In a shallow dish, season the flour with salt and pepper. Coat the chops with the flour mixture.

4 Heat the oil in a large skillet on high heat. Cook the chops until golden, about 2 minutes per side. Remove the meat from the skillet and place in an ovenproof casserole.

5 Drain off all but 1 tbsp (15 mL) oil from the skillet. Add the leeks and sauté until softened slightly, about 5 minutes.

6 Add the garlic and orange rind and sauté for 1 minute. Pour in the tomato sauce and stock and bring to boil.

7 Pour the sauce over the meat. Cover and bake for 40 to 50 minutes, or until the veal is tender. Remove the orange rind and season to taste with salt and pepper. Sprinkle with dill before serving.

Serves 4

veal chops with citrus sauce

For a special dinner, try this easy recipe for veal chops with a fresh and tangy sauce. Substitute pork chops, if desired.

1 tbsp	olive oil	15 mL
1 tbsp	butter	15 mL
4	rib veal chops, about 1 inch (2.5 cm) thick	4

citrus sauce

½ cup	orange juice	125 mL
¼ cup	lime juice	50 mL
1 tsp	lemon juice	5 mL
½ tsp	granulated sugar	2 mL
1 tsp	dried tarragon	5 mL
½ cup	whipping cream	125 mL

1 Preheat the oven to 425° F (220° C).
2 In a large skillet, melt the oil and butter on medium-high heat. Place the chops in the pan (in batches if necessary) and brown on both sides, about 2 minutes per side.
3 Remove the chops to an ovenproof baking dish and bake for 12 minutes.
4 Place the chops on a serving dish and reserve in a warm place. Discard the fat from the skillet. To make the sauce, pour in the orange, lime and lemon juices, sugar, tarragon and any accumulated veal juices. Reduce until 2 tbsp (25 mL) remains.

5 Add the whipping cream and reduce until slightly thickened. Pour this sauce over the chops.
Serves 4

quick tips for leftover meat

- Always trim all the fat off any leftover meat. It doesn't taste good the second time around.
- Cut leftover rare beef into thin slices. Layer them on a serving dish with finely chopped onion, sliced tomatoes and chopped pickles and drizzle each layer with a spoonful of vinaigrette.
- As an alternative to pâté, potted meats are quickly made with leftovers, and they should keep for up to one week in the refrigerator. In a food processor or by hand, finely chop 8 oz (250 g) leftover cooked meat, chicken or fish. Melt ¼ cup (50 mL) butter in a small skillet on low heat. Add the meat, a pinch of dried marjoram, a pinch of nutmeg and salt and pepper to taste. Simmer very gently for 3 minutes. Stir in 2 tbsp (25 mL) brandy. Pour into a small container and refrigerate, covered, until needed. Serve with toast or crackers.

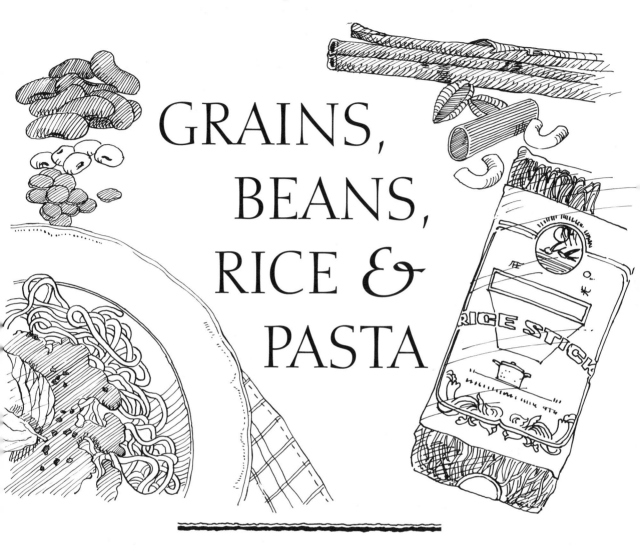

chapter seven

GRAINS, BEANS, RICE & PASTA

*G*rains, beans, rice and pasta are the chic ingredients of the
nineties. I like them because they are easy to cook, healthy,
tasty and inexpensive; they also adapt well to all sorts of cuisines.
Nutritionally, they contain complex carbohydrates, which are
absorbed and burned more quickly by the body than proteins, and
they have a high fibre content.

99

GRAINS

It's a shame that more people today aren't turned on to cheap, tasty, quick-cooking, nutritious grains. Much to our nutritional detriment, we consume far fewer grains than our ancestors. Our problem lies in our lack of knowledge about how to use grains to their best advantage. They cook as fast as rice or pasta, they make excellent one-dish meals combined with meat and vegetables and they are a welcome change from more traditional side dishes.

tips

- The value in grains – wheat, rice, barley, oats, rye and corn – is in their fibre, which helps to regulate blood sugar and lower cholesterol.
- Grains are also complex carbohydrates, providing calories that are fat-free and easy to burn.
- Buy grains from a store that has a good turnover to make sure you get the freshest possible.
- Store grains in a cool place in an airtight container.

mixed grain pilaf

The grains can be varied in this healthy, interesting dish. Use red lentils instead of green and/or brown rice instead of wild rice for a different combination.

¼ cup	olive oil	50 mL
1	red onion, chopped	1
2	cloves garlic, chopped	2
⅓ cup	wild rice	75 mL
⅓ cup	barley	75 mL
1 tsp	dried thyme	5 mL
4 cups	water	1 L
½ cup	green lentils	125 mL
½ cup	bulgur	125 mL
	Salt and freshly ground pepper to taste	
2 tbsp	finely chopped parsley	25 mL

1 Heat the oil in a large pot on medium heat. Add the onion and garlic and sauté until the onion is soft, about 3 minutes.
2 Stir in the wild rice and barley and coat with the oil. Sprinkle with the thyme and pour in the water. Bring to a boil, cover, lower the heat and simmer for 25 minutes.
3 Add the lentils and bulgur to the pot and simmer together for 25 to 30 minutes more, covered, adding more water if the mixture seems too dry. Season with the salt and pepper. Stir in the parsley.
Serves 6 as a side dish

100

warm lentil salad with feta and spicy vinaigrette

Serve the lentils hot from the pot, tossed with the spicy vinaigrette and vegetables. Alternatively, toss the lentils with the vinaigrette while still hot, cool and serve at room temperature.

1½ cups	green lentils	375 mL
2	cloves garlic, finely chopped	2
1 tsp	dried oregano	5 mL

spicy vinaigrette

	Grated rind and juice of 1 lemon	
½ tsp	paprika	2 mL
¼ tsp	cayenne pepper	1 mL
½ tsp	ground cumin	2 mL
½ cup	olive oil	125 mL

2 tbsp	finely chopped mint	25 mL
2 tbsp	finely chopped parsley	25 mL
2	tomatoes, chopped	2
4	green onions, chopped	4
3 oz	feta cheese, crumbled	90 g
	Salt and freshly ground pepper to taste	

1 In a medium pot, cover the lentils with plenty of cold water. Bring to a boil and add the garlic and oregano. Cover and simmer on low heat until lentils are tender, 35 to 45 minutes.

2 To make the vinaigrette, in a small bowl, combine the lemon rind and juice, paprika, cayenne, cumin and olive oil.

3 Drain the lentils and toss in a large bowl with the vinaigrette, mint, parsley, tomatoes and green onions.

4 Stir in the feta cheese and season with salt and pepper.

Serves 4 as a side dish

lentils

Lentils come in two colours – red and green. The red lentils have no outer husk and therefore cook very quickly to a purée. The green lentils retain their outer seed coat and take a little longer to cook, but they have much more texture and are especially good in salads.

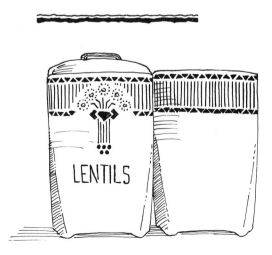

lemony lentils

A great side dish for any grilled fish or meat. It has depth of flavour but is not hot.

1 tbsp	vegetable oil	15 mL
1	onion, chopped	1
2	cloves garlic, finely chopped	2
1 tbsp	finely chopped fresh ginger	15 mL
1 tsp	dried chili flakes	5 mL
2 tsp	ground cumin	10 mL
1	½-inch (1.25 cm) cinnamon stick	1
1 cup	green lentils	250 mL
2 cups	water	500 mL
1	bay leaf	1
2	slices lemon, about ½-inch (1.25 cm) thick	2
	Salt and freshly ground pepper to taste	

1 In a medium pot, heat the oil over medium heat. Add the onion, garlic, ginger, chili flakes, cumin and cinnamon stick. Sauté for about 2 minutes, or until fragrant.
2 Add the lentils and cook, stirring, until the lentils are coated with the seasoning mixture.
3 Add the water, bay leaf and lemon slices. Bring to a boil, reduce the heat to medium-low, cover and simmer for 35 to 45 minutes, or until the lentils are tender. Season well with salt and pepper. Drain off any excess water and remove the lemon slices and bay leaf before serving.
Serves 4 as a side dish

savoury couscous

Buy quick-cooking couscous; it cooks in five minutes, which is hours less than the regular kind. Serve as a side dish with Corsican Chicken (see page 74) or any highly flavoured fish or meat dish.

1½ cups	chicken stock or water	375 mL
1 tbsp	olive oil	15 mL
1 tbsp	lemon juice	15 mL
½ cup	finely diced carrot	125 mL
½ cup	finely diced zucchini	125 mL
1 cup	quick-cooking couscous	250 mL
	Salt and freshly ground pepper to taste	

1 In a medium pot, bring the stock, olive oil, lemon juice, carrot and zucchini to a boil.
2 Add the couscous, stirring until it is coated with the liquid. Cover the pot and remove from the heat. Let stand for 5 minutes, then fluff with a fork. Serve immediately.
Serves 4 as a side dish

couscous

Couscous is a grain-sized pasta indigenous to North Africa. It is made by grinding semolina and water together, cooking
it before drying and crushing it into small
pellets. Its taste is similar to pasta, and it
is wonderful served with spicy meats and
vegetables.

chickpea couscous

*Another quick couscous recipe that can be
served as a main course if you add cooked
chicken or meat. If you can find the Middle
Eastern hot harissa (chili) sauce sold in
tubes or jars, serve it separately. Otherwise
serve Tabasco on the side.*

2 tbsp	butter	25 mL
1	onion, chopped	1
1 tsp	ground cumin	5 mL
½ tsp	paprika	2 mL
1½ cups	chicken stock or water	375 mL
1 cup	quick-cooking couscous	250 mL
1 cup	cooked or canned chickpeas	250 mL
1 cup	frozen or cooked peas	250 mL
	Salt and freshly ground pepper to taste	
3 tbsp	finely chopped parsley	45 mL

1 In a medium pot on high heat, melt the
butter. When it sizzles, add the onion and
sauté until it is softened, about 2 minutes.
2 Stir in the cumin and paprika. Add the
chicken stock, bring to a boil and add the
couscous all at once, stirring constantly.
Add the chickpeas and peas, cover and
remove from the heat. Let stand for
5 minutes, or until all the stock is
absorbed.
3 Season with salt and pepper and stir in
the parsley.
Serves 4 as a side dish

tabbouleh

A Middle Eastern salad. Try it with hamburgers or lamb chops or as a nutritious lunch. It's a good portable dish for picnics, too. If you make it the day before, fold in the tomatoes just before serving.

1½ cups	**bulgur**	**375 mL**
1½ cups	**boiling water**	**375 mL**
2	**tomatoes, chopped**	**2**
6	**green onions, chopped**	**6**
¼ cup	**finely chopped parsley**	**50 mL**
¼ cup	**finely chopped mint**	**50 mL**
¼ cup	**olive oil**	**50 mL**
	Juice of 1 lemon	
	Salt and freshly	
	ground pepper to taste	

1   Place the bulgur in a large bowl and cover with the boiling water. Let sit for 30 minutes. Fluff with a fork. Cool.
2   Add the tomatoes, green onions, parsley, mint, olive oil and lemon juice. Toss together. Season well with salt and pepper. Add more lemon juice to taste.
Serves 6 as a side dish

bulgur

Bulgur is the Turkish name for cracked wheat berries. It is known as the rice of the Middle East. To make bulgur, the wheat berries are partially roasted and then cracked. As a result, the bulgur can be soaked in boiling water instead of being cooked. Its fine nutty flavour complements meat and poultry dishes.

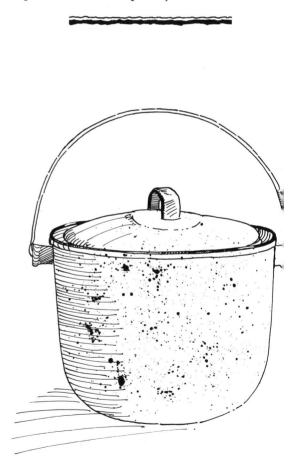

BEANS

Beans are high in protein, minerals and fibre and low in fat. They have a proven ability to lower cholesterol and regulate blood sugar.

tips

■ Dried beans are high in fibre – ½ cup (125 mL) cooked beans contains 4 grams of dietary fibre and supplies about 8 grams of protein (about the same as 2 oz/60 g meat). Beans are also a good source of calcium, magnesium, zinc, niacin, thiamine, riboflavin and iron.

■ Dried beans take too long to cook if you are in a hurry, but canned kidney beans, chickpeas and white kidney beans (cannellini) work well in most dishes.

brazilian black beans

Serve as a side dish with Easy Grilled Chicken (see page 62) or Veal Chops with Citrus Sauce (see page 98). You can use any canned or cooked beans to make this tasty side dish.

2 tbsp	vegetable oil	25 mL
1	large onion, chopped	1
3	cloves garlic, finely chopped	3
2 cups	chopped tomato	500 mL
2 cups	cooked or canned black beans	500 mL
1 tsp	ground cumin	5 mL
¼ tsp	cayenne pepper	1 mL
1 tbsp	red wine vinegar	15 mL
	Salt to taste	
¼ cup	sour cream	50 mL

1 Heat the oil in a large skillet over medium heat. Add the onion and garlic and sauté until the onion is softened, about 5 minutes.

2 Add the tomato, beans, cumin, cayenne and vinegar. Stir together and bring to a boil. Lower the heat and simmer, uncovered, for 5 minutes. Season well with salt. Serve with a dollop of sour cream on each serving.

Serves 4 as a side dish

sausage and cannellini bean salad

This salad can be served as a first course or main dish. It is also great as a buffet dish. Use canned cannellini beans (white kidney beans) or canned red kidney beans.

Turn this into a warm salad by preparing the beans in advance and sautéing the sausages at the last minute. Toss the hot sausages with the cold beans – sensational!

4 tbsp	olive oil	50 mL
1 lb	spicy Italian sausages	500 g
¼ cup	chopped fresh basil	50 mL
3 tbsp	lemon juice	45 mL
3	shallots or green onions, chopped	3
3	tomatoes, chopped	3
¼ cup	cider or	50 mL
	balsamic vinegar	
2 cups	cooked cannellini beans, or	500 mL
	1 19-oz (540 mL) can, drained	
	Salt and freshly	
	ground pepper to taste	
2 cups	spinach, washed and dried	500 mL

1 In a large skillet, heat 2 tbsp (25 mL) oil on medium heat. Sauté the sausages until brown and cooked through, about 15 minutes. Cool and cut into thin slices.

2 In a medium bowl, whisk together the basil, lemon juice, shallots, tomatoes, vinegar and 2 tbsp (25 mL) oil.

3 In a large bowl, combine the sausages with the beans. Pour the dressing over, seasoning well with salt and pepper.

4 Arrange the spinach on a large platter or individual plates. Spoon the bean mixture in the centre.

Serves 4 as a main dish

how to cook dried beans

Method 1: The Overnight Soak. Cover the beans with three times their volume of cold water and soak overnight or for 12 hours at room temperature. The beans usually double in size after soaking. Replace the soaking liquid with enough fresh water to cover the beans. Cover and simmer until tender, from 45 to 90 minutes.

Method 2: The Quick Soak. In a pot, place the beans in twice their volume of cold water. Bring to a boil and boil for 2 minutes. Remove from heat, cover and soak for 1 hour. Replace the soaking liquid with enough fresh water to cover the beans. Cover and simmer until tender, from 45 to 90 minutes.

Rack of lamb Provençale, page 88

Pork tenderloin with apples and brandy, page 94

Warm lentil salad with feta, page 101

Linguine with seafood, page 112

Roasted red potatoes, page 129

Apple ginger crisp, page 164

Derby squares, page 176

Sabayon, page 178

RICE

It used to be that rice was always the same boring white side dish. But as we become more globally aware and better travelled, many different varieties of rice are appearing.

Rice makes an excellent starch dish, it's a great gravy absorber and it can be combined with vegetables and meat to make a one-dish meal.

tips

■ Long-grain rice has a slender grain. When cooked, it should be light and fluffy.

■ Short-grain rice has a slightly round grain. It is used in puddings and risottos because it absorbs lots of liquid and becomes creamy and sticky.

■ Brown rice retains an outer layer of fibrous bran. It has a nutty, creamy texture and takes twice as long to cook as white rice.

■ Wild rice is not technically a rice at all; it is a grass. But its flavour is so compatible with rice that they are often cooked together. The price is high because no method has been found to grow and harvest it on a large scale.

pilau rice

A luxurious Indian rice dish. In India, it might come garnished with edible silver paper! To make this dish extra special, use basmati rice. The slender, elongated grain has a nutty taste. Fold in an assortment of cooked vegetables before serving, if desired.

2 tbsp	vegetable oil	25 mL
1	small onion, sliced	1
½ tsp	turmeric	2 mL
6	whole cloves	6
2	1-inch (5 cm) sticks cinnamon	2
1	bay leaf	1
½ tsp	ground cardamom	2 mL
2 cups	basmati or long-grain rice	500 mL
3½ cups	chicken stock or water	875 mL
	Salt to taste	

1 In a large pot, heat the oil on medium heat. Add the onion and cook, stirring occasionally, until brown around the edges, about 10 minutes.

2 Add the turmeric, cloves, cinnamon, bay leaf, cardamom and rice. Stir until the rice is coated with the oil.

3 Add the stock, bring to a boil, then cover. Reduce the heat to low and cook for 15 to 20 minutes, or until the rice is tender. Season with salt if necessary.

Serves 6 to 8 as a side dish

cardamom

Cardamom is an expensive spice because each pod must be snipped off the bushes by hand. If you buy the spice in pod form (which will stay fresh longer than the ground spice), remove the husks before using the seeds. Use cardamom in Indian cooking or to flavour mulled wine, fruit salads and Turkish coffee. To flavour rice dishes, you can throw in the whole pod and remove it before eating. Ground cardamom is used in baking.

chili powder

Chili powders vary in strength and flavour, depending on who makes them. The powder is not a spice but a mixture of several different peppers and other spices such as cumin. Look for brands that are manufactured in Mexico or the southwestern U.S. for a more authentic flavour. To spike up the milder commercial varieties, add extra cayenne and cumin.

indonesian fried rice

A great dish for leftover rice. Use up leftover chicken, seafood or beef and mix in cooked vegetables, too. Served with a salad, this makes a nutritious and tasty meal.

2 tbsp	vegetable oil	25 mL
1	onion, finely chopped	1
1	clove garlic, finely chopped	1
1 tsp	finely chopped fresh ginger	5 mL
2 tsp	chili powder	10 mL
1 cup	diced cooked chicken	250 mL
3 cups	cooked rice	750 mL
½ cup	frozen or cooked peas	125 mL
2 tbsp	soy sauce	25 mL
	Salt and freshly ground pepper to taste	
½ cup	peanuts	125 mL

1 Over high heat, heat the oil in a large skillet. Sauté the onion, garlic and ginger until the onion has softened, about 1 minute. Stir in the chili powder and cook, stirring, for 1 minute longer.

2 Add the chicken, cooked rice, peas and soy sauce and stir well. Season with the salt and pepper and continue to cook, stirring, until the rice is hot. Add the peanuts and toss together before serving.

Serves 3 or 4 as a main dish

spicy rice southern style

This tangy sausage- and tomato-based rice can be served as a main dish or as a side dish with barbecued or fried foods. Increase the Tabasco or cayenne for a spicier kick. To make this rice even more substantial, cooked shrimp and/or chopped ham can be added.

1 tbsp	vegetable oil	15 mL
2	hot Italian sausages, sliced	2
2 cups	chopped onion	500 mL
1 cup	chopped green pepper	250 mL
½ cup	chopped celery	125 mL
2	cloves garlic, finely chopped	2
1½ cups	puréed canned tomato	375 mL
½ cup	water	125 mL
½ tsp	dried thyme	2 mL
½ tsp	cayenne pepper or Tabasco	2 mL
1 cup	long-grain rice	250 mL
½ tsp	salt	2 mL
2 tbsp	finely chopped fresh parsley	25 mL

1 Heat the oil in large skillet on medium heat. Add the sausages and sauté until partially cooked, about 5 minutes.

2 Stir in the onion, green pepper, celery and garlic. Sauté for about 3 minutes, or until the vegetables are softened.

3 Add the tomato, water, thyme and cayenne and bring to a boil. Sprinkle in the rice and salt. Cover tightly; turn the heat to low and cook for 20 to 25 minutes, or until the rice is tender. Garnish with the parsley before serving.

Serves 4 as a main dish

coconut spinach rice

This delightful-looking and tasty dish goes with all spicy food. If possible, buy canned coconut milk or use creamed coconut (in a bar) diluted with water. Both are available in Chinese and Indian food stores.

1 cup	long-grain rice	250 mL
2 cups	chopped spinach	500 mL
1 cup	coconut milk	250 mL
1 cup	water	250 mL
½ tsp	salt	2 mL

1 Place all the ingredients in a medium pot. Cover and bring to a boil.

2 Turn the heat to low and simmer for 20 minutes, or until the rice is cooked. Fluff before serving.

Serves 4 as a side dish

PASTA

There is nothing faster than throwing together a quick, tasty sauce and pouring it over noodles. By keeping a selection of pasta in the cupboard and using ingredients on hand in the refrigerator (often leftover meat or vegetables spiced up with some chili peppers and lots of garlic), you can prepare an instant meal.

tips

■ Keep lots of dried noodles on hand in several different shapes. I prefer the imported dried Italian pastas because they tend to have more flavour than the domestic varieties and they don't get mushy.

■ I seldom use fresh pasta because the quality varies and it is not suitable for heavy or spicy sauces. When I do buy fresh pasta, I use it with creamy, light sauces, which are absorbed by the noodles.

fettuccine with mushrooms and lemon

The mushrooms bring out the lemon flavour in this recipe. You can combine a selection of wild mushrooms with the fresh mushrooms, if you wish. This sauce is very good with fresh pasta, which absorbs the lemon flavour especially well.

1 lb	fettuccine	500 g
1/3 cup	olive oil	75 mL
1/3 cup	butter	75 mL
1 lb	mushrooms, sliced	500 g
	Grated rind and juice of 2 lemons	
1/2 cup	whipping cream	125 mL
	Salt and freshly ground pepper to taste	
2 tbsp	finely chopped parsley	25 mL
1/4 cup	grated Parmesan cheese	50 mL

1 Bring a large pot of salted water to a boil and add the fettuccine. Boil until the pasta is *al dente*, 3 to 5 minutes for fresh; about 10 minutes for dried. Drain well.

2 Meanwhile, in a large skillet, heat the olive oil and butter on high heat. Add the mushrooms and lemon rind and sauté, stirring often, until the mushrooms just begin to become limp, about 3 minutes.

3 Add the lemon juice and simmer for 2 minutes. Add the cream and simmer for another 2 minutes, or until slightly thickened. Season with salt and pepper. Stir in the parsley.

4 Toss the sauce with the pasta and serve the cheese separately.

Serves 4 as a main dish

parmesan cheese

The finest Parmesan in the world is Parmigiano Reggiano. It is made according to strict rules in the province of Emilia Romagna in Italy. Only milk from the region may be used, and the cheese is monitored for eighteen months before it is sold. In fact, when you buy Parmigiano Reggiano, it will be stamped with its name and the month of production. There is no substitute for it. The grated Parmesan cheese sold in cans has much less taste and texture. Buy wedges of fresh Parmesan and grate it as you need it. Try shaving it into salads and hot vegetable dishes for a real flavour boost.

butterfly pasta with basil

This pasta is perfect for a summer meal. Serve it with Herbed Roasted Chicken (see page 72) or any veal or pork dish.

8 oz	farfalle (butterfly pasta)	250 g
¼ cup	slivered fresh basil leaves	50 mL
2 tbsp	olive oil	25 mL
	Salt and freshly	
	ground pepper to taste	

1 Bring a large pot of salted water to a boil. Add the farfalle and boil until *al dente*, 10 to 12 minutes. Drain well.

2 Stir in the basil leaves, olive oil, salt and pepper. Toss together.

Serves 4 as a side dish

linguine with seafood

Serve pasta and sauce in a large bowl on the table and let people help themselves. Vary the seafood according to your tastes. If you want a vegetarian version, sauté mushrooms and peppers instead of seafood and add to tomato sauce. Grated Parmesan traditionally is not offered with seafood dishes.

2 tbsp	olive oil	25 mL
3	shallots or green onions, chopped	3
3	cloves garlic, chopped	3
1 tsp	grated lemon rind	5 mL
2 tbsp	chopped parsley	25 mL
12	large shrimps	12
12	scallops	12
	Salt and freshly ground pepper to taste	
1/2 cup	white wine	125 mL
2 lb	mussels	1 kg
1	28-oz (796 mL) can tomatoes	1
1/2 tsp	red chili pepper flakes	2 mL
1/4 cup	shredded fresh basil	50 mL
1 lb	linguini	500 g

1 In a large skillet, heat olive oil over medium-high heat. Add shallots and garlic. Sauté for 1 minute, or until softened slightly. Add lemon rind, parsley, shrimps and scallops. Sauté until shrimps just turn pink and scallops are translucent, about 1 to 2 minutes. Remove from skillet with a slotted spoon. Season with salt and pepper.

2 Add white wine to skillet, bring to a boil and add mussels. Cover and steam mussels until they open, about 3 minutes. Remove mussels from skillet and reserve with shrimps and scallops. (Discard any mussels that do not open.) Remove meat from half of mussels, leaving remainder in their shells.

3 Meanwhile, drain tomatoes and chop, reserving juice. Add tomatoes, juice and chili flakes to skillet and bring to a boil. Stir in 2 tbsp (25 mL) basil and simmer for 10 minutes to combine flavours. Season with salt and pepper. Sauce can be made ahead to this point.

4 When ready to serve, bring a large pot of salted water to a boil. Add pasta and boil until *al dente,* about 10 to 12 minutes. Drain well.

5 Return seafood to sauce, sprinkle with remaining basil and reheat. Toss with pasta and serve.

Serves 4

nut and herb sauce for pasta

This is a basic recipe that can be put together in minutes. If you want it to taste like pesto, use fresh basil, pine nuts and Parmesan or pecorino, another hard Italian cheese (the harder the cheese the better this recipe will work). Experiment with what you have available. If you want a different flavour, use walnuts, parsley, Romano cheese and replace the olive oil with walnut oil. Toss the sauce with your favourite pasta – use ½ cup (125 mL) of sauce per 1 cup (250 mL) of cooked pasta. The sauce is also delicious on new potatoes and with fish or chicken. Store the sauce in the refrigerator in small jars. Cover with a thin layer of oil before putting on the lids. It should keep for two weeks.

1	clove of garlic	1
½ cup	fresh herbs	125 mL
2 tbsp	shelled nuts	25 mL
4 oz	cheese, grated	60 g
½ cup	olive oil	125 mL
	Salt to taste	

1 Chop the garlic and herbs finely.
2 Use a food processor or a mortar and pestle to grind the nuts until smooth. If using a food processor, process so that the mixture retains some texture. Mix in the herbs and garlic.

3 Stir in the grated cheese and then whisk in the olive oil a little at a time, until the sauce thickens. Add salt to taste.
Makes 1½ cups (375 mL)

linguine with olive paste

A favourite pasta for those who like earthy food. The sauce is scrumptious with pasta. Serve this as an appetizer followed by a strongly flavoured main course such as Baked Lamb Provençal (see page 88).

1 lb	linguine	500 g
2	cloves garlic, peeled	2
½ cup	black olives, pitted	125 mL
1	anchovy	1
3 tbsp	coarsely chopped parsley	45 mL
½ cup	olive oil	125 mL
	Freshly ground pepper to taste	

1 Bring a large pot of salted water to a boil. Add the linguine and boil until the pasta is *al dente*, about 10 minutes. Drain well.
2 Meanwhile, in a food processor or blender, chop the garlic, olives, anchovy and parsley.
3 With the machine running, add the oil through the feed tube. Season with pepper.
4 Toss the sauce with the pasta.
Serves 6 as an appetizer

113

penne with spicy sausage and tomato sauce

A hot spicy dish that makes a super supper in the winter time. Look for real Italian sausages for an authentic flavour.

2 tbsp	olive oil	25 mL
1 lb	hot Italian sausages	500 g
1	onion, chopped	1
1	28-oz (796 mL) can tomatoes, drained and chopped	1
1 tsp	dried basil	5 mL
½ tsp	dried chili flakes	2 mL
	Salt and freshly ground pepper to taste	
1 lb	penne	500 g

1 In a large skillet, heat the olive oil over medium-high heat. Add the sausages and cook until browned on all sides, about 5 minutes. Remove from the heat.

2 Add the onion to the skillet and sauté until softened, about 2 minutes. Add the tomatoes, basil and chili flakes. Simmer for 5 minutes.

3 Slice the sausages into ¼-inch (5 mm) slices. Add to the tomato sauce and simmer together for 5 more minutes, or until the sausages are cooked through. Season with salt and pepper.

4 Meanwhile, bring a large pot of salted water to a boil and add the penne. Boil until the penne is *al dente*, about 10 minutes. Drain well and toss with the sauce.

Serves 4 as a main dish

pasta shapes

Although there is no hard and fast rule, sauces that contain pieces of meat or vegetables are generally served with hollow pastas such as penne, or a shape that can catch the pieces, such as the corkscrew-shaped fusilli or shells. Thinner sauces, such as tomato, go with long strands of pasta (spaghetti or linguine); seafood sauces are almost always served with long pasta. Fresh pasta is used with sauces that need to be absorbed by the pasta, such as the creamy Alfredo sauce.

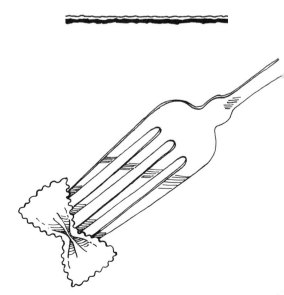

penne and prosciutto

A simple full-flavoured dish that can be put together in minutes. If prosciutto is unavailable, use any smoked ham.

1 lb	penne	500 g
2 tbsp	olive oil	25 mL
2 tbsp	butter	25 mL
1	red pepper, diced	1
4 oz	prosciutto, sliced	125 g
10 oz	fresh spinach, chopped	300 g
1 tsp	dried rosemary	5 mL
	Salt and freshly	
	ground pepper to taste	
½ cup	grated Parmesan cheese	125 mL

1 Bring a large pot of salted water to a boil and add the penne. Boil until the pasta is *al dente*, 12 to 15 minutes. Drain well.

2 Meanwhile, in a large skillet, heat the olive oil and butter over high heat. Add the red pepper and sauté until the pepper is slightly softened and browned, about 2 minutes.

3 Add the prosciutto and sauté for 1 minute. Add the spinach and sauté until the spinach is slightly wilted, about 1 minute. Season with the rosemary, salt and pepper.

4 Toss the pasta with the sauce and sprinkle with Parmesan cheese before serving.

Serves 4 as a main dish

Pasta needs to retain its surface starch for the sauce to stick to it. Rinsing removes that starch. Rinse pasta only when it is going to be used in a salad.

Pasta should be served in a bowl so the sauce is contained by the sides. If you don't have pasta bowls, try soup bowls. To eat long pasta, twirl it around your fork. No self-respecting Italian would be seen using a spoon, except to mix the sauce and pasta together.

I never sprinkle cheese on seafood sauces; it detracts from the taste of the fresh seafood.

prosciutto

Prosciutto is an air-cured, salted ham in which the meat is surrounded by a thin ribbon of mellow fat. It ranges in colour from orangey pink to deep red. Prosciutto is wonderful eaten raw with melon or figs and it will contribute a concentrated flavour to a cooked pasta sauce. The finest prosciutto comes from the Parma region of Italy where, it is said, the quality of the air produces a superior flavour and texture.

spaghetti carbonara

A traditional, easy bacon-and-egg pasta that kids like a lot. It uses a few simple ingredients that most people always have on hand. In this dish the heat of the pasta cooks the eggs. For a truly authentic taste, use Italian pancetta, a rolled bacon that is not smoked.

1 lb	spaghetti	500 g
2 tbsp	olive oil	25 mL
8 oz	bacon, diced	250 mL
1	clove garlic, finely chopped	1
1	small onion, chopped	1
4	eggs, beaten	4
1 cup	grated Parmesan cheese	250 mL
	Salt and freshly ground pepper to taste	
2 tbsp	finely chopped parsley	25 mL

1 Bring a large pot of salted water to a boil and add the spaghetti. Boil until the pasta is *al dente*, about 10 minutes. Drain well.
2 Meanwhile, heat the olive oil in a large skillet on medium heat. Add the bacon and cook until crisp, pouring off the fat as it accumulates. Add the garlic and onion and sauté until the onion softens, about 5 minutes.

3 In a large serving bowl, beat the eggs and cheese together. Add the drained hot pasta and toss until the pasta is coated with the egg mixture. Add the bacon/onion mixture and toss again. Season liberally with salt and freshly ground pepper and garnish with the parsley.
Serves 4 as a main dish

chinese fried noodles with chicken and vegetables

You'll love the crispy noodles combined with the flavourful chicken and veggies. It is a quick one-dish supper and it can be stretched with leftover vegetables or meats.

Chinese recipes look more complicated than they are. This dish should take only 30 minutes from beginning to end.

2	single boneless chicken breasts, skin removed	2

marinade

½ tsp	granulated sugar	2 mL
2 tsp	white vinegar	10 mL
1 tsp	dry white wine	5 mL

1 tbsp	soy sauce	15 mL
1/3 cup	vegetable oil	75 mL
8 oz	Chinese egg noodles or	250 g
	angelhair (capellini) noodles, cooked	
1 tbsp	finely chopped fresh ginger	15 mL
1	clove garlic, finely chopped	1
1	medium zucchini, diced	1
1/2 cup	snow peas, slivered	125 mL
1/2 cup	diced red pepper	125 mL
2	green onions, slivered	2

seasoning sauce

2/3 cup	chicken stock	150 mL
1/2 tsp	granulated sugar	2 mL
1 tsp	rice vinegar	5 mL
1 tsp	cornstarch	5 mL
1 tsp	sesame oil	5 mL
1 tbsp	soy sauce	15 mL

1 Slice the chicken breasts into thin strips.

2 To make the marinade, in a small bowl, combine 1/2 tsp (2 mL) sugar with the white vinegar, wine and 1 tbsp (15 mL) soy sauce. Marinate the chicken in this mixture for 15 minutes at room temperature.

3 In a large skillet or wok over high heat, heat 1/4 cup (50 mL) oil. When the oil is very hot, add the cooked noodles in a single layer and cook until the bottom is browned, about 3 minutes. Lift the noodles around the edges with a spatula so they don't stick. Slide the noodles onto a plate and invert back into the skillet to fry the second side. When crisp and brown (about 2 minutes), remove to a serving platter.

4 Heat the remaining 2 tbsp (25 mL) oil in the same skillet. Add the ginger and garlic. Stir-fry for 30 seconds, then add the drained chicken, zucchini, snow peas and red pepper. Stir-fry until the chicken has lost its pinkness, about 2 minutes. Mix in the green onions.

5 In a small bowl, stir together all the ingredients for the seasoning sauce and add to the contents of the skillet. Bring to a boil and spoon over the noodles. Serve at once.

Serves 4 as a main dish

oriental noodle dishes

In Southeast Asia and China, noodles are a staple food. Soft egg noodles, wheat noodles made with or without egg, dried and fresh rice noodles and noodles made from the starch of bean sprouts are all used in everyday cooking. They can be stir-fried, deep-fried, boiled or simmered in soups. Dried rice noodles must be soaked or boiled before being used in most recipes, although they can be deep-fried directly from the dried state. The most readily available substitute for Chinese wheat noodles are Italian angelhair (capellini) noodles.

warm noodle salad

This is a good dish for people who have vegetable and herb gardens because it is best made with fresh herbs, and any vegetable combination will work. The sauce can also be used as a marinade for barbecued chicken and pork. Serve it with Grilled Scallops (see page 53). If fish sauce is unavailable, use chopped anchovies.

sauce

2 tbsp	chopped fresh mint	25 mL
2 tbsp	chopped fresh basil	25 mL
2 tbsp	chopped fresh coriander	25 mL
1 tsp	finely chopped green chili	5 mL
	Grated rind and juice of 1 lime	
3 tbsp	fish sauce	45 mL
2/3 cup	chicken stock	150 mL
2 tbsp	red wine vinegar	25 mL
2 tbsp	vegetable oil	25 mL
1 tbsp	grated fresh ginger	15 mL
1	clove garlic, minced	1
pinch	granulated sugar	pinch

8 oz	angelhair (capellini) noodles	250 g
2 tbsp	vegetable oil	25 mL
4 oz	mushrooms, sliced	125 g
1 cup	snow peas, cut in half lengthwise	250 mL
1½ cups	sliced asparagus	375 mL
3	green onions, cut into 1-inch (2.5 cm) slices	3
½ cup	cherry tomatoes, cut in half	125 mL
2 tbsp	chopped fresh coriander	25 mL

1 In a small bowl, combine all the sauce ingredients. Reserve.

2 Bring a large pot of water to a boil. Add the noodles and boil for about 4 minutes, or until *al dente*. Drain and toss with 1 tbsp (15 mL) oil.

3 In a large skillet or wok, heat the remaining 1 tbsp (15 mL) oil on high heat. Add the mushrooms, snow peas, asparagus, green onions and tomatoes. Stir-fry until crisp-tender, about 1 minute. Stir in the noodles and toss everything together.

4 Pour the sauce into the skillet and bring to a boil. The noodles should absorb most of the sauce. Serve on a platter garnished with 2 tbsp (25 mL) coriander.

Serves 4 as a side dish

fish sauce

This salty liquid is used throughout Southeast Asia in place of the better-known Chinese soy sauce. It is the liquid extract that comes from salting and fermenting small fish like anchovies. It tastes much better than it sounds, and it does not deepen the colour of dishes the way soy sauce does. It is now available in Chinese supermarkets and in some supermarkets and health-food stores.

chapter eight

VEGETABLES

*V*egetables can play a starring role in a meal. There is so much choice that you can highlight a different vegetable every night of the week. Vegetables can also be prepared quickly (even root vegetables, which require longer cooking, can be cut into small pieces when time is of the essence). I like to serve two vegetables with a main dish, for both taste and colour. Garnet red cabbage sitting beside cream-coloured cauliflower or the greenest beans makes a visual presentation that has your mouth watering even before you begin eating.

tips

- When boiling root vegetables, place them in a pot and cover with cold water. Cover, bring to a boil and simmer until tender. Drain the vegetables, then put the pot back on the turned-off element to help the vegetables dry off (shake the pot occasionally).

- Green vegetables should be boiled for as short a time as possible to help preserve their colour. Bring a large pot of water to a boil, then add the vegetables and return to a boil. Boil, uncovered, just until crisp-tender, drain, then refresh with about 2 cups (500 mL) cold water to stop the cooking. If you are going to reheat the vegetables later, cool them right down by running cold water over them until they are cold. This will help them retain their colour and texture.

asparagus with cream and cheese

This is a decadent dish to include in a special meal. Serve as a first course with French bread and chilled white wine or as a vegetable side dish with plain grilled meats.

2 lb	asparagus	1 kg
2 tbsp	butter	25 mL
2 tbsp	chopped green onion	25 mL
½ cup	whipping cream	125 mL
1 tsp	lemon juice	5 mL
⅔ cup	grated Parmesan cheese	150 mL

1 Cut the asparagus into 2-inch (5 cm) lengths. Bring a large pot of water to the boil and add the asparagus. Cook for 1 minute. Drain and refresh with cold water.

2 Melt the butter in a large skillet on medium heat. Add the green onion and asparagus. Sauté together for 1 minute.

3 Add the cream and simmer slowly, uncovered, until the cream has thickened, about 5 minutes. Fold in the lemon juice and Parmesan and simmer together until the cheese has melted.

Serves 6

asparagus with yogourt hollandaise

A good way to serve asparagus when you want to keep the calories down. Unadorned asparagus itself has about 75 calories per 1 pound (500 g).

1 lb	asparagus, cooked until crisp-tender	500 g
1	egg yolk	1
1 tsp	dried tarragon	5 mL
1 tbsp	lemon juice	15 mL
¼ cup	low-fat plain yogourt	50 mL
2 tsp	butter	10 mL
	Salt and freshly ground pepper to taste	

1 Bring a large pot of water to a boil. Add the asparagus and cook until crisp-tender, 2 to 5 minutes. Drain and refresh with cold water. Reserve.

2 Meanwhile, in a small pot on low heat, whisk together the egg yolk, tarragon and 1 tsp (5 mL) lemon juice until the yolk thickens slightly.

3 Whisk in the yogourt and continue to cook until the mixture thickens slightly, about 3 minutes. Do not boil. Beat in the butter until it is incorporated. Season to taste with the remaining lemon juice, salt and pepper. Serve over the warm asparagus or serve on the side.

Serves 3 to 4

asparagus

Snap the woody ends off the asparagus before cooking. If the stalks are fat, peel off the tough outer skin with a vegetable peeler. If the stalks are pencil-thin, they do not need to be peeled.

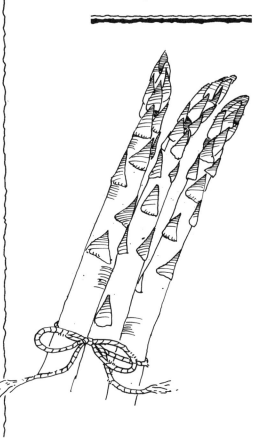

stir-fried asparagus

An easy, quick asparagus dish.

1 lb	asparagus	500 g
1 tbsp	vegetable oil	15 mL
1	slice fresh ginger	1
2 tbsp	chicken stock	25 mL
1 tbsp	soy sauce	15 mL
1 tsp	sesame seeds	5 mL

1 Peel the asparagus stalks if they are thick. Cut the asparagus into 2-inch (2.5 cm) lengths.
2 In a large skillet, heat the vegetable oil and ginger on high heat. Add the asparagus and stir-fry until the asparagus is coated with the oil.
3 Add the chicken stock, cover and cook for 2 minutes or until the asparagus is crisp-tender. Stir in the soy sauce and sesame seeds.
Serves 4

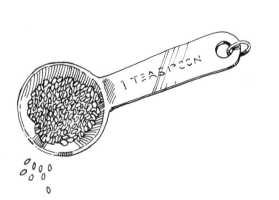

nutty sprouts

Substitute hazelnuts or almonds for macadamia nuts, if macadamias are unavailable.

1 lb	Brussels sprouts	500 g
¼ cup	butter	50 mL
12	macadamia nuts, halved	12
	Salt and freshly	
	ground pepper to taste	

1 Bring a large pot of water to a boil. Add the sprouts and boil for about 10 minutes, or until crisp-tender. Drain and refresh with cold water.
2 Melt the butter in a large skillet on high heat. Sauté the nuts for about 1 minute, or until golden. Add the sprouts, reheat and season well with salt and pepper.
Serves 4

macadamia nuts

Macadamia nuts are considered the world's best by nut gourmets because of their crisp texture and faintly sweet flavour. They are also one of the most expensive. They are actually seeds and originally came from Australia. Macadamias are now grown commercially in Hawaii.

brussels sprouts with prosciutto

Try this savoury dish with the Thanksgiving or Christmas turkey.

1 lb	Brussels sprouts	500 g
1 tbsp	olive oil	15 mL
2 oz	prosciutto, chopped	60 g
	Freshly ground pepper to taste	

1 Bring a large pot of salted water to a boil. Add the Brussels sprouts and cook for 10 minutes, or until tender. Drain and refresh with cold water.
2 Heat the olive oil in a large skillet on medium-high heat. Add the prosciutto and sauté until crisp, about 2 minutes. Add the sprouts and sauté until hot. Season with the pepper before serving.
Serves 4

preparing brussels sprouts

Wash the sprouts, removing any yellow leaves. Trim off the bottoms. With a knife, make a cross on the bottom of each stem to help promote even cooking.

stir-fried broccoli

Broccoli can be purple or green. The purple broccoli is more delicate. This basic stir-fry can be used with any green vegetable.

1	bunch broccoli	1
2 tbsp	vegetable oil	25 mL
1 tbsp	finely chopped fresh ginger	15 mL
1	clove garlic, finely chopped	1
2	green onions, chopped	2
2 tbsp	water	25 mL
2 tbsp	oyster sauce	25 mL
1 tsp	sesame oil	5 mL

1 Separate the broccoli into florets; peel the stems and cut into thin slices.
2 Heat the oil in a large skillet or wok on high heat. Add the ginger, garlic and green onions and stir-fry for 30 seconds. Add the broccoli stems and stir-fry for 1 minute. Add the florets and stir-fry for 1 minute longer. Splash in the water and boil until it evaporates, about 1 minute.
3 Stir in the oyster sauce and sesame oil. Cook together for 1 minute, stirring occasionally.
Serves 4

carrot, zucchini and potato shreds

A simple stir-fry that provides both the starch and the veggies in one dish.

2	baking potatoes, peeled	2
2	small carrots, peeled	2
2	medium zucchini	2
2 tbsp	butter	25 mL
1 tsp	dried basil	5 mL
	Salt and freshly ground pepper to taste	

1 Grate the potatoes. Rinse with cold water, drain well and pat dry.

2 Grate the carrots and zucchini and combine with the potatoes.

3 Melt the butter in a large skillet on medium-high heat. When sizzling, add the vegetables and sauté for 2 minutes. Add the basil, lower the heat to medium, cover and simmer for 7 to 10 minutes, or until the vegetables are tender. Season with salt and pepper.

Serves 4

cauliflower curry

In India it is the tradition to cook all vegetables until they are mushy. I prefer crisp-tender cauliflower. Serve with Easy Grilled Chicken (see page 62) or as a vegetarian main dish with rice.

2	onions, peeled	2
1	clove garlic, peeled	1
1 tbsp	ground ginger	15 mL
2 tsp	ground cumin	10 mL
1 tsp	dried chili flakes	5 mL
1 tsp	turmeric	5 mL
1 cup	plain yogourt	250 mL
1	head cauliflower	1
2 tbsp	vegetable oil	25 mL
2	whole cloves	2
1	2-inch (5 cm) stick cinnamon	1
1 cup	water	250 mL

1 Slice 1 onion and reserve.

2 In a food processor or blender, combine the remaining onion, garlic, ginger, cumin, chili flakes and turmeric. Grind to a paste. Stir in the yogourt.

3 Cut the cauliflower into small florets. Marinate in the yogourt mixture for 15 minutes.

4 Heat the oil in a large skillet on medium-low heat. Add the reserved sliced onion and sauté until golden-brown, about 10 minutes.

5 Stir in the cloves, cinnamon, cauliflower and marinade. Sauté for 2 minutes, or until everything is coated with the marinade.

6 Add the water, bring to a boil and cover. Simmer for 20 minutes, or until the cauliflower is tender.

Serves 4

cauliflower

Look for heavy cream-coloured heads of cauliflower with no brown spots. The florets should be tightly closed. If the florets feel loose, the cauliflower is overripe. Store cauliflower in the refrigerator, uncovered, for up to five days.

cabbage with grainy mustard

A fast, piquant cabbage dish that is delicious with duck, pork chops or sausages. Add sliced onion with the garlic for a slightly different taste.

1	small head cabbage	1
2 tbsp	olive oil	25 mL
1	clove garlic, finely chopped	1
1 tbsp	water	15 mL
2 tbsp	coarse-grained mustard	25 mL
	Salt and freshly ground pepper to taste	

1 Thinly slice the cabbage.

2 Heat the olive oil in a large skillet on high heat. Add the cabbage and garlic and sauté until the cabbage is coated with the oil and beginning to wilt, about 3 minutes.

3 Stir in the water and mustard. Cover the skillet, turn the heat to low and simmer for 5 minutes, or until the cabbage is crisp-tender. Season with salt and pepper.

Serves 4

eggplant salsa

This salsa can be served as a vegetable side dish or over grilled swordfish or tuna or any grilled chicken dish. It can also be served cold as part of an antipasta platter.

1	large eggplant, peeled	1
1 tsp	salt	5 mL
2 tbsp	olive oil	25 mL
1	onion, chopped	1
3	cloves garlic, finely chopped	3
1 tsp	ground cumin	5 mL
1 tsp	ground coriander	5 mL
1	chili pepper, chopped, optional	1
3	tomatoes, peeled, seeded and chopped	3
2 tbsp	balsamic or cider vinegar	25 mL
	Salt and freshly ground pepper to taste	
2 tbsp	chopped fresh coriander	25 mL

1 Cut the eggplant into ½-inch (1.25 cm) cubes. Place in a colander and sprinkle with the salt. Leave to drain for 15 minutes. Pat dry with paper towels.
2 Heat the olive oil in a large skillet on high heat. Add the eggplant cubes and sauté until softened, about 2 minutes. Remove from the pan.
3 Turn the heat to low and add the onion and garlic to the skillet. Sauté until the onion softens and turns slightly brown, about 10 minutes. Stir in the cumin, coriander and chili pepper.

4 Return the eggplant to the skillet. Add the tomatoes and vinegar, cover and cook until the eggplant is cooked through, about 10 minutes. Season with salt and pepper and sprinkle with coriander.
Serve 4 to 6

pungent eggplant

Serve this colourful, earthy dish as a vegetarian main course or as a side dish. Accompany it with spicy pappadums (available at Indian food stores) fried crisp in a little vegetable oil. Triangles of warm pita bread or steamed brown rice are also excellent accompaniments. Garlic chili paste is available at Chinese grocery stores.

1	eggplant, peeled and diced	1
1 tsp	salt	5 mL
¼ cup	vegetable oil	50 mL
1	leek (dark-green leaves removed), sliced	1
2	cloves garlic, finely chopped	2
8 oz	small mushrooms	250 g
1	red pepper, diced	1

sauce

¼ cup	tomato sauce	50 mL
2 tbsp	dry white wine	25 mL
1 tbsp	soy sauce	15 mL

1 tbsp	red wine vinegar	15 mL
1 tsp	granulated sugar	5 mL
1/3 cup	chicken stock	75 mL
1 tsp	garlic chili paste, or	5 mL
	1/2 tsp (2 mL) cayenne pepper	

1 Sprinkle the eggplant with the salt, place in a colander and drain for 15 minutes. Pat dry.

2 Heat 2 tbsp (25 mL) oil in a wok or large skillet on high heat. Stir-fry the eggplant until browned. Add the remaining oil, leek, garlic, mushrooms and pepper. Cook until the pepper is crisp-tender, about 3 minutes.

3 Meanwhile, in a small bowl, combine the tomato sauce, wine, soy sauce, vinegar, sugar, stock and garlic chili paste. Pour the sauce over the vegetables and bring to a boil. Cook until slightly thickened, about 5 minutes, stirring occasionally. Serve hot.

Serves 4 as a side dish

eggplant

Look for eggplant that is glossy, firm to the touch and unblemished. Store it in the refrigerator for up to one week.

Eggplant can have bitter juices. The best way to release them is to salt slices or cubes and let them sit for 15 to 30 minutes. The salt will draw out the juices. Pat the eggplant dry before using. (The smaller Italian eggplants and the long skinny Chinese ones have no bitter-ness and do not need to be salted. They are best stir-fried or cut in half and barbecued or baked.

leeks parmesan

Serve as a first course or as a vegetable with any simple main course. This dish can be made ahead and browned when needed.

1 cup	chicken stock	250 mL
4	leeks (dark-green leaves removed)	4
2 tbsp	butter	25 mL
1/2 cup	grated Parmesan cheese	125 mL
	Salt and freshly ground pepper to taste	
1/2 tsp	grated nutmeg	2 mL

1 In a medium skillet, bring the stock to a boil on high heat. Add the leeks, turn the heat down to medium and simmer for 10 to 15 minutes, or until the leeks are tender. Remove the leeks to an ovenproof dish just large enough to hold them.

2 Reduce stock to 1/4 cup (50 mL). Beat in the butter and Parmesan. Heat to bubbling and season with salt, pepper and nutmeg. Pour the sauce over the leeks.

3 Just before serving, brown the dish under the broiler, making sure the cheese doesn't burn.

Serves 4

garlicky mashed potatoes

The mellow creaminess of the cooked garlic gives the potatoes a special lift.

4	baking potatoes, peeled and cut into quarters	4
8	cloves garlic, unpeeled	8
¼ cup	butter	50 mL
½ cup	milk	125 mL
	Salt and freshly ground pepper to taste	

1 Place the potatoes and garlic in a pot of cold water to cover. Bring to a boil. Simmer until the potatoes are tender, about 10 minutes. Drain and press the garlic cloves out of their skins.

2 With a potato masher or electric beater, mash the potatoes and garlic together. Beat in the butter and milk. Season with salt and pepper.

Serves 4

new potatoes dijon style

A mustardy, spicy potato dish. Little red potatoes have the best flavour, but white ones can be substituted. Serve with Southern Fried Chicken (see page 66).

2 lb	red potatoes, unpeeled	1 kg
½ cup	whipping cream	125 mL
3 tbsp	Dijon mustard	45 mL
¼ cup	finely chopped chives	50 mL
	Salt and freshly ground pepper to taste	

1 Place the potatoes in a large pot and cover with cold water. Bring to a boil and boil for about 10 minutes, or until just tender. Drain well and cool slightly.

2 Slice the potatoes thinly and return to the pot.

3 In a small bowl, beat together the cream, mustard and chives. Pour over the potatoes and simmer together over low heat, stirring occasionally, for 5 minutes, or until the sauce thickens and is partially absorbed by the potatoes. Season well with salt and pepper.

Serves 6

roasted red potatoes

Red potatoes have a soft, melting texture when baked.

1 lb	mini red potatoes	500 g
2 tbsp	olive oil	25 mL
1 tbsp	chopped fresh rosemary,	15 mL
	or 1 tsp (5 mL) dried	
	Salt and freshly ground pepper to taste	

1 Preheat oven to 400 F (200 C).

2 Peel a strip of skin around centre of each potato. Place potatoes in roasting pan and toss with oil. Sprinkle on rosemary, salt and pepper.

3 Bake, stirring occasionally, 35 to 45 minutes, or until potatoes are tender and golden.

Serves 4

potato creole

Creole cooking was trendy even fifty years ago (this recipe comes from my husband's grandmother). Serve with New Zealand Hamburgers (see page 89).

¼ cup	vegetable oil	50 mL
3	potatoes, peeled and sliced	3
1	onion, sliced	1
2 cups	chopped tomatoes	500 mL
	Salt and freshly ground pepper to taste	
1 tsp	dried thyme	5 mL
pinch	cayenne pepper	pinch

1 Heat the oil in a large skillet on medium heat. Add the potatoes and onion and sauté for 10 minutes.

2 Add the tomatoes, salt, pepper, thyme and cayenne. Bring to a boil, then reduce the heat, cover and simmer for 30 minutes, or until the potatoes are tender and the sauce has thickened.

Serves 4

potatoes

New potatoes have not built up the starch of an older potato. With their waxy texture, they are the best potatoes for salads. Don't store them in the refrigerator, but keep them in a cool dark place (refrigerator dampness will cause the potatoes to sprout). New potatoes are at their best when very fresh. Try to eat them within two days of buying.

Oval-shaped baking potatoes (Idaho or russet) have a different texture from new potatoes. When they are cooked, the flesh is floury rather than waxy. These potatoes are best for mashing, frying and baking.

"low-calorie" french fries

These oven-baked French fries deliver the taste and look of the deep-fried ones but not the calories. Don't peel the potatoes; there is lots of nutrition in the skin.

3	baking potatoes	3
2 tbsp	olive or vegetable oil	25 mL
	Salt and freshly	
	ground pepper to taste	
pinch	paprika	pinch

1 Preheat the oven to 400° F (200° C).

2 Slice the potatoes to look like thick French fries.

3 Place the oil in a large bowl and toss the potatoes with it. Season with the salt, pepper and paprika. Lay the potatoes on an oiled baking sheet.

4 Bake for 15 minutes, turn the potatoes over and bake for another 15 minutes, or until a deep golden-brown.

Serves 4

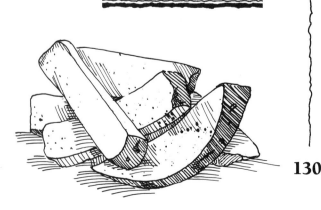

sautéed potatoes with rosemary

This is one of my favourite potato dishes when rosemary is fresh.

4	baking potatoes,	4
	peeled and thinly sliced	
2 tbsp	butter	25 mL
2 tbsp	olive oil	25 mL
2 tbsp	chopped fresh rosemary,	25 mL
	or 2 tsp (10 mL) dried	
	Salt and freshly	
	ground pepper to taste	

1 In a large pot, cover the potatoes with water and bring to a boil. Boil for about 5 minutes, or until the potatoes are crisp-tender. Drain well.

2 In a large skillet on medium-high heat, heat the butter and oil until sizzling. Add the potatoes and sprinkle with rosemary. Sauté the potatoes, turning frequently, until they become brown and crusty, about 10 minutes. Season with salt and pepper before serving.

Serves 4 to 6

stir-fried red cabbage

Red cabbage dishes are traditionally cooked for several hours, but this quick stir-fried version leaves a little crunch in the cabbage without sacrificing any taste.

½	head red cabbage	½
1	tart apple	1
2 tbsp	olive oil	25 mL
2 tbsp	balsamic or cider vinegar	25 mL
1 tbsp	red currant jelly	15 mL
	Salt and freshly ground pepper to taste	

1 Thinly slice the cabbage. Peel and slice the apple.
2 Heat the oil in a large skillet on high heat. Add the cabbage and apple and stir-fry until the cabbage is limp, about 5 minutes.
3 Stir in the balsamic vinegar and red currant jelly. Bring to a boil. Season well with salt and pepper.

Serves 4

cumin-scented spinach

This delicately scented spinach dish can be served with Pork Tenderloin with Spicy Applesauce (see page 94) or Braised Veal Chops with Leeks and Orange (see page 97). Its slightly Asian flavour goes well with fish dishes, too.

10 oz	fresh spinach	300 g
2 tbsp	butter	25 mL
1 tsp	ground cumin	5 mL
1 tsp	lime juice	5 mL
	Salt and freshly ground pepper to taste	

1 Wash the spinach. Place the spinach and the water that clings to its leaves in a pot. Cover and cook on medium heat until the spinach is just wilted, about 5 minutes.
2 Drain the spinach, rinse with cold water and squeeze out the excess water.
3 Melt the butter in the same pot on medium heat. Stir in the cumin and spinach. Sauté until hot. Season with the lime juice, salt and pepper.

Serves 4

radicchio ragu

Radicchio and Belgian endive lose their bitterness when slowly simmered and take on a mellow, subtle flavour and texture. Serve with veal chops or any grilled chicken dish.

2	Belgian endives	2
1	head radicchio	1
2 tbsp	olive oil	25 mL
1 tbsp	balsamic or wine vinegar	15 mL
	Salt and freshly ground	
	pepper to taste	

1 Thickly slice the endives diagonally. Cut the radicchio into four and pull apart.
2 Heat the olive oil in a large skillet on medium heat. Add the endives and radicchio. Stir to coat with the oil. Turn the heat to low, cover pan and simmer vegetables for 20 to 25 minutes, or until very soft.
3 Pour the vinegar over top. Boil until the liquid evaporates, about 2 minutes. Season with salt and pepper.
Serves 4

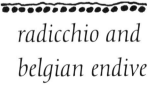

radicchio and belgian endive

Radicchio looks like a tiny curled-up red cabbage. Its deep ruby colour adds life to a salad. It is similar to Belgian endive in taste. They both have a slightly bitter tang, but radicchio is less crisp. When cooked it turns darker and takes on a lingering mellow flavour.

When buying heads of Belgian endive, look for short white leaves with yellow tips. (The green-tipped leaves can be bitter.)

scalloped tomatoes

This dish is best made with fresh tomatoes, but you can use chopped canned tomatoes. It is great served with Light-Style Meatloaf (see page 83) or a plain hamburger.

¼ cup	butter	50 mL
1	onion, chopped	1
2	cloves garlic, finely chopped	2
4 cups	chopped, peeled tomatoes	1 L
2 tbsp	chopped fresh basil, or	25 mL
	2 tsp (10 mL) dried	
1 tsp	granulated sugar	5 mL
	Salt and freshly	
	ground pepper to taste	
1 cup	fresh breadcrumbs	250 mL
¼ cup	grated Parmesan cheese	50 mL

1 Preheat the oven to 350° F (180° C).
2 Heat 2 tbsp (25 mL) butter in a large skillet on medium heat. Add the onion and

garlic and sauté until the onion is softened, about 2 minutes.

3 Add the tomatoes, basil, sugar, salt and pepper. Stir everything together. Remove from the heat and place in a buttered 8-cup (2 L) ovenproof casserole.

4 Top with the breadcrumbs and Parmesan cheese. Dot with the remaining 2 tbsp (25 mL) butter. Bake, uncovered, for 20 minutes, or until bubbling.

Serves 4

root vegetable gratin

A rich, creamy gratin that can include Jerusalem artichokes, kohlrabi or any other root vegetable. Cut the vegetables the same size for even cooking.

2	**white turnips, peeled and diced**	2
2	**parsnips, peeled and diced**	2
2	**baking potatoes, peeled and diced**	2
2	**carrots, peeled and diced**	2
2 tbsp	**butter**	25 mL
½ tsp	**grated nutmeg**	2 mL
1 tbsp	**chopped fresh rosemary,**	15 mL
	or 1 tsp (5 mL) dried	
	Salt and freshly	
	ground pepper to taste	
½ cup	**whipping cream**	125 mL
¼ cup	**finely chopped parsley**	50 mL

1 Preheat the oven to 400° F (200° C).

2 In a large pot, cover the turnips, parsnips, potatoes and carrots with water and bring to a boil. Boil for 5 to 7 minutes, or until the vegetables are crisp-tender. Drain and refresh with cold water.

3 Melt the butter in a 9-inch (23 cm) ovenproof baking dish. Stir in the vegetables and sprinkle with the nutmeg, rosemary, salt and pepper. Pour the cream over.

4 Bake, uncovered, for 25 to 30 minutes, or until the vegetables are soft and creamy. Sprinkle with parsley before serving.

Serves 4 to 6

turnips and rutabagas

Rutabagas are often called turnips. However, they are not the same vegetable. Rutabagas are waxed yellow globes with golden flesh and an earthy flavour. Many people say they don't like them, but try them braised in butter, glazed or mashed with potatoes – sensational! Turnips are the purple-topped, white-fleshed softball-sized roots; they are milder in flavour than rutabagas but are used in the same way.

Choose rutabagas and turnips that feel heavy for their size. They should keep for several months if stored in a cool place.

grated zucchini

A simple, terrific dish to serve with fish.

3	zucchini	3
	Salt	
3 tbsp	butter	45 mL
	Freshly ground pepper to taste	

1 Grate the zucchini and salt lightly. Leave for 15 minutes. Squeeze out all the liquid.
2 In a skillet, heat the butter on high heat until sizzling. Toss in the zucchini and sauté for 2 minutes. Season with pepper.
Serves 4

zucchini latkes

This lighter version of potato latkes goes especially well with poultry dishes. You can serve them alone as a nibbly before dinner or top them with sour cream and smoked salmon.

1 lb	zucchini	500 g
1	small onion	1
2	eggs	2
2 tbsp	all-purpose flour	25 mL
	Salt and freshly ground pepper to taste	
2 tbsp	finely chopped parsley	25 mL
¼ cup	vegetable oil	50 mL

1 In a large bowl, grate the zucchini and onion together, discarding any liquid that collects.
2 Stir in the eggs, flour, salt, pepper and parsley.
3 Heat 2 tbsp (25 mL) oil in a large skillet on medium heat. Spoon the batter into the oil in 2 tbsp (25 mL) portions and flatten. Cook for 1 to 2 minutes per side, or until brown. Repeat with the remaining oil and batter.
Makes about 12 latkes

quick tips for leftover vegetables

- Cover leftover vegetables with stock and cream and purée in a food processor or blender for instant soup. Season with herbs or curry powder.
- Combine 2 cups (500 mL) chopped cooked vegetables with 1 egg and enough flour to achieve a pancake-batter consistency. Add 1 tbsp (15 mL) chopped nuts for crunch and fry like pancakes.
- Chop up leftover cooked vegetables and use in frittatas or quiches, or as a filling for omelettes or crêpes.

chapter nine

SALADS

Salads are useful additions to the repertoire of someone who doesn't want to spend a lot of time in the kitchen. With creativity and a few basic ground rules, you can create super salads in no time at all.

To make your salads more interesting, try combining a selection of lettuces – such as Boston, Romaine and radicchio – with a vinaigrette dressing. Or try lightly cooked vegetables or grated root vegetables with a spicy dressing. Great salads can be made from leftovers, too. Poultry, meat or fish can be combined with greens and dressed with a spicy vinaigrette for an instant supper.

tips

- A rule of thumb for salad-making is to use three times as much oil as vinegar or other acid. If you use 2 tbsp (15 mL) vinegar, you will need 6 tbsp (60 mL) oil.
- I prefer olive oil for salad dressings because of its subtle taste, but any vegetable oil can be substituted.
- Red or white wine vinegar is most often used in salad dressings, but substituting any citrus juice will give your vinaigrette a special tart, fresh taste.
- Egg yolks, mustard or cream can be used to help a salad dressing emulsify and thicken.
- Salads can be served as a main course or as a side dish. They can be the appetizer before a meal, or the "palate cleanser" after the main course.

crisp pear salad with sesame ginger dressing

The dressing for this salad is low in fat and has Oriental overtones. It would also be delicious served over chicken salad. Sesame oil is available at many supermarkets.

2 cups	spinach	500 mL
1	small head Boston lettuce	1
2	green onions, slivered	2
2	Japanese pears or green apples, peeled and sliced	2

sesame ginger dressing

2 tsp	soy sauce	10 mL
2 tbsp	vegetable oil	25 mL
¼ cup	lime juice	50 mL
2 tsp	brown sugar	10 mL
1 tsp	sesame oil	5 mL
1 tsp	grated fresh ginger	5 mL
1 tsp	Dijon mustard	5 mL

1 Remove the stems from the spinach. Tear the spinach and lettuce into bite-sized pieces and place in a salad bowl. Sprinkle with the green onions and Japanese pears and toss.

2 In a small bowl, whisk together the dressing ingredients. Toss with the salad.

Serves 4

japanese pears

Crisp Japanese apple/pears (properly known as Asian pears), are round large yellow to green pears that are crunchy and juicy. They are excellent in salads because they can be cut into paper-thin slices. They can be stored in the refrigerator for up to one month.

asparagus salad with creamy orange vinaigrette

The creamy orange vinaigrette tastes superb over pencil-thin asparagus. Pile the asparagus on a platter and coat with the sauce. Serve as a first course or as a side salad with fish dishes.

1 lb	asparagus, peeled	500 g

creamy orange vinaigrette

1	egg yolk	1
1 tbsp	lemon juice	15 mL
Grated rind and juice of 1 orange		

½ tsp	Dijon mustard	2 mL
¼ cup	olive oil	50 mL
2 tbsp	finely chopped chives or green onion tops	25 mL

1 Bring a pot of water to a boil. Add the asparagus and cook until crisp-tender, about 3 minutes. Drain and cool under cold running water.

2 To make the vinaigrette, in a food processor or blender, combine the egg yolk, lemon juice, orange rind and juice and mustard. With the machine running, pour the olive oil slowly through the feed tube. (If the dressing is too thick, thin with extra orange juice.)

3 Place the asparagus on a serving platter and drizzle with the dressing. Sprinkle with the chives.

Serves 4

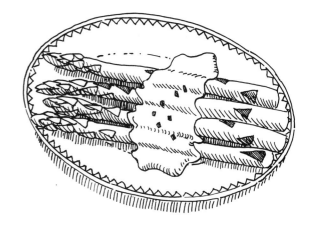

boston lettuce with leek vinaigrette

A good first-course salad to serve before a more intricate main course. You can use green onions instead of leeks.

leek vinaigrette

1	small leek	1
2 tbsp	wine vinegar	25 mL
½ cup	olive oil	125 mL
	Salt and freshly ground pepper to taste	
1	head Boston lettuce	1

1 Wash the leek and cut off the dark-green leaves. Cut the leaves into julienne strips. Reserve. Chop the white part of the leek finely.

2 In a small bowl, whisk together chopped leek and vinegar. Whisk in the olive oil and season with salt and pepper.

3 Arrange the lettuce on a flat platter. Scatter with julienned leek and pour over enough dressing to moisten the lettuce.
Serves 4

red and green summer slaw

The combination of red and green cabbage makes an unusual and attractive cole slaw. This is a recipe for the sweet/sour type of cole slaw and not the creamy variety. It can be made up to two days ahead.

2 cups	shredded red cabbage	500 mL
2 cups	shredded green cabbage	500 mL
1 cup	shredded fennel bulb	250 mL
2	green onions, chopped	2

vinaigrette

¼ cup	white vinegar	50 mL
pinch	dry mustard	pinch
1	clove garlic, minced	1
2 tsp	granulated sugar	10 mL
1 tsp	salt	5 mL
	Freshly ground pepper to taste	
⅓ cup	vegetable oil	75 mL

1 In a large bowl, toss the cabbages, fennel and onions.

2 To make the vinaigrette, in a small bowl, whisk together the vinegar, mustard, garlic, sugar, salt and pepper; slowly whisk in the oil.

3 Pour over vegetables and toss again. Taste and adjust the seasoning.
Serves 4

herb garlic toast

Creative accompaniments to salads can turn them into more exciting fare.

To make herb garlic toast, in a small bowl, combine ½ cup (125 mL) olive oil with 2 finely chopped cloves garlic, and 2 tsp (10 mL) dried herbs of your choice (eg., thyme, tarragon, rosemary). Brush onto slices of bread and bake for 20 minutes at 325° F (160° C), until golden-brown. Spread goat cheese on the toasts, if desired.

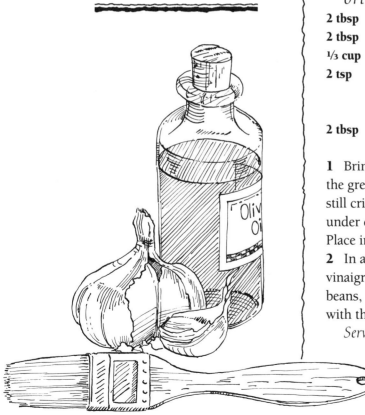

green bean salad

We have this salad at all our family celebrations. It looks fresh and light, it's easy to make in large quantities and everyone loves the flavour. It can be left to marinate in the refrigerator overnight, if you want to make it ahead.

1 lb	green beans, trimmed	500 g

oriental vinaigrette

2 tbsp	soy sauce	25 mL
2 tbsp	rice or wine vinegar	25 mL
⅓ cup	vegetable oil	75 mL
2 tsp	sesame oil	10 mL
	Pepper to taste	
2 tbsp	toasted sesame seeds	25 mL

1 Bring a large pot of water to a boil. Add the green beans and cook until tender but still crisp, about 3 minutes. Drain and cool under cold running water. Drain again. Place in a salad bowl.

2 In a small bowl, whisk together the vinaigrette ingredients. Toss with the green beans, adding pepper as needed. Garnish with the sesame seeds.

Serves 4

winter salad

This salad tastes fresh and summery, although it is made with vegetables and fruits that are available in the winter. To toast pine nuts, place them on a baking sheet and bake at 375° F (190° C) for 5 minutes.

10 oz	fresh spinach	300 g
1	bunch watercress, stems removed	1
3	oranges	3
1	red onion, chopped	1
4 oz	mushrooms, sliced	125 g
½ cup	toasted pine nuts	125 mL

citrus vinaigrette

2 tbsp	lemon juice	25 mL
2 tbsp	lime juice	25 mL
1 tsp	Dijon mustard	5 mL
1 tsp	dried tarragon	5 mL
½ cup	olive oil	125 mL
	Salt and freshly ground pepper to taste	

1 Strip the spinach leaves from the ribs and tear into bite-sized pieces. Place in a large salad bowl. Add the watercress leaves.
2 Remove the rind and white pith from the oranges and slice them into rounds ⅛ inch (3 mm) thick. Cut each round in half. Add to the spinach. Sprinkle with the red onion, mushrooms and pine nuts.
3 In a small bowl, combine the lemon juice and lime juice with the mustard and

tarragon. Slowly whisk in the oil. Season with salt and pepper. Toss with the salad just before serving.
Serves 6 to 8

summer salad with brie croutes

Experiment with different combinations of salad leaves, using arugula and radicchio with Boston lettuce, for example, or combining more readily available lettuces such as Boston, leaf, romaine, and red leaf for colour. For a variation, use goat cheese instead of Brie. I often make extra toasts and pass them around separately.

4	½-inch (1.25 cm) slices French bread	4
¼ cup	olive oil	50 mL
2 oz	Brie cheese	60 g
6 cups	mixed salad greens	1.5 L

balsamic vinaigrette

2 tbsp	balsamic vinegar	25 mL
½ tsp	Dijon mustard	2 mL
1 tbsp	chopped fresh basil, or 1 tsp (5 mL) dried	15 mL
½ cup	olive oil	125 mL
	Salt and freshly ground pepper to taste	

1 Preheat the oven to 350° F (180° C).
2 Brush the bread slices on both sides with ¼ cup (50 mL) oil. Place the slices on a baking sheet and bake for 15 to 20 minutes, or until the bread is light-brown.
3 Cut the Brie into thin slices and place on top of the toasts. Reserve.
4 Place the salad greens in a bowl.
5 To make the vinaigrette, whisk together the vinegar, mustard, basil and remaining ½ cup (125 mL) oil in a small bowl. Season with salt and pepper. Pour over the greens and toss. Divide among 4 plates.
6 Bake the Brie toasts for 5 minutes, or until the cheese is melted. Grind fresh pepper over the toasts. Serve 1 per person alongside the salad.
   Serves 4

balsamic vinegar

Balsamic vinegar is a mellow, russet vinegar from northern Italy. It is aged for many years in barrels of different woods. The longer it is aged, the better it becomes and the more it costs. There is no real substitute for the sweet/tart taste of this vinegar (which is now available in most supermarkets), but if it is unavailable, use a mild rice or cider vinegar.

carrots with cumin vinaigrette

A good salad with stews or curries, or serve as part of a mixed hors d'oeuvre.

6	**large carrots, grated**	6
2	**green onions, chopped**	2

cumin vinaigrette

2 tbsp	**lemon juice**	**25 mL**
1 tsp	**ground cumin**	**5 mL**
1 tsp	**liquid honey**	**5 mL**
⅓ cup	**olive oil**	**75 mL**
	Salt and freshly	
	ground pepper to taste	

1 Combine the carrots and green onions on a flat serving dish.
2 To make the vinaigrette, whisk together the lemon juice, cumin and honey in a small bowl. Slowly whisk in the olive oil. Season with salt and pepper. Pour the vinaigrette over the carrots and marinate for 30 minutes at room temperature.
   Serves 4 to 6

orange and red onion salad

A simple, quick, colourful salad that is great as a buffet dish or served with poultry. Try serving it with your Christmas turkey.

4	seedless oranges	4
1	red onion, thinly sliced	1
1 cup	black olives	250 mL

lemon vinaigrette

1 tbsp	lemon juice	15 mL
½ tsp	Dijon mustard	2 mL
⅓ cup	olive oil	75 mL
2 tbsp	finely chopped fresh parsley	25 mL
	Salt and freshly ground pepper to taste	

1 Over a bowl, remove the skin and white pith from the oranges, reserving any juice. Cut the oranges into thin slices and place on a flat serving dish. Top with the red onion and scatter the olives over top.

2 To make the vinaigrette, mix together the lemon juice and mustard in a small bowl. Pour in any juice from the oranges. Whisk in the olive oil. Stir in the parsley. Season with salt and pepper and pour over the salad.

Serves 6

how to peel an orange

Take a sharp serrated knife and, starting at the top of the orange, carefully saw off the skin and the white pith and membrane underneath. Continue to saw, turning the orange around and around. The skin should come off in one continuous strip. Slice the orange into circles or divide into segments.

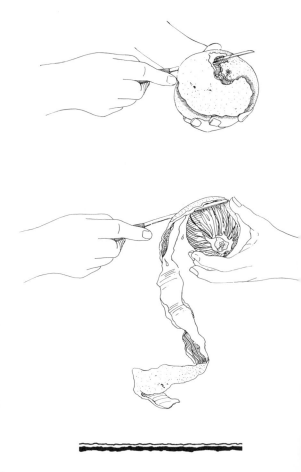

three-pepper cheese salad

An appetizing riot of colours that can be presented as a tangle on a serving platter or in neat sections on individual salad plates. You can substitute roasted peppers. This can be made up to twelve hours ahead.

4 oz	mozzarella, shredded	125 g
1	green pepper, sliced in thin strips	1
1	red pepper, sliced in thin strips	1
1	yellow pepper, sliced in thin strips	1
1	red onion, thinly sliced	1

italian vinaigrette

1 tsp	Dijon mustard	5 mL
2 tbsp	white wine vinegar	25 mL
1½ tsp	chopped fresh oregano, or	7 mL
	½ tsp (2 mL) dried	
⅓ cup	olive oil	75 mL
	Salt and freshly	
	ground pepper to taste	

1 Place the mozzarella in a bowl with the peppers and onion.
2 To make the vinaigrette, whisk together the mustard, vinegar and oregano in a small bowl. Whisk in the olive oil. The mixture should thicken slightly. Season with salt and pepper.
3 Pour the vinaigrette over the peppers.
Serves 4

roasting peppers

To roast peppers, cut the peppers in half and remove the seeds. Place the peppers, skin side up, on a baking sheet. Broil about 3 inches (7.5 cm) from the heat until the skin is blackened. Place the peppers in a plastic bag or paper bag. Leave for 10 minutes, or until the skin loosens and the peppers are cool enough to handle. Peel off the skin and slice the peppers. To preserve roasted peppers, pack them in jars, cover them with olive or vegetable oil and refrigerate. They should keep for about three months.

onions

The best onions for eating raw are mild Spanish onions, the sweet Georgia-bred Vidalia onions (only available in the spring and summer), red onions (which are so pretty in salads) and the large white Bermuda onions. To make them taste even milder, lightly sprinkle chopped or sliced raw onions with salt and let them sit for 15 minutes. This draws out the strong juices. Pat them dry before using. Alternatively, marinate raw onions in vinegar for about 30 minutes, then discard the vinegar before tossing the onions in a salad.

tomato salad

It is not necessary to use vinegar in plain tomato salads – they have enough acid of their own.

4	tomatoes	4
2 tbsp	chopped fresh basil, or	25 mL
	2 tsp (10 mL) dried	
¼ cup	olive oil	50 mL
	Salt and freshly	
	ground pepper to taste	

1 Slice the tomatoes. Lay on a flat serving dish. Sprinkle with the basil and olive oil and season to taste with salt and pepper.
Serves 4

quick tomato salads

- Slice a red or Spanish onion into thin rings and scatter over sliced tomatoes. Drizzle with olive oil and a sprinkling of wine vinegar.
- Intersperse tomato slices with cucumber slices and drizzle with olive oil and a squeeze of lemon.
- Top sliced tomatoes with rounds of mozzarella cheese and drizzle with olive oil and a little wine vinegar. Season well with salt and pepper.
- Cut tomatoes into chunks and mix them with equal amounts of cucumber, melon and avocado, all cut roughly the same size. Toss with Basic Vinaigrette (see page 152).

papaya and avocado salad

To make this into a light supper dish, mix cooked shrimp into the salad. Use mango instead of papaya for a flavour change.

ginger lime vinaigrette

2 tbsp	lime juice	25 mL
1 tsp	liquid honey	5 mL
¼ tsp	ground ginger	1 mL
1 tsp	Dijon mustard	5 mL
⅓ cup	olive oil	75 mL
1	head Boston lettuce	1
1	papaya	1
1	avocado	1
3	green onions, chopped	3

1 To make the vinaigrette, whisk together the lime juice, honey, ginger and mustard in a small bowl. Whisk in the olive oil.
2 Tear the lettuce into large pieces and place in a salad bowl. Peel the papaya, scooping out the seeds. Reserve 1 tbsp (15 mL) seeds for a garnish. Slice the papaya thinly and place in the salad bowl.

3 Peel the avocado and slice thinly. Toss with the papaya. Sprinkle the salad with the green onions.

4 Pour the vinaigrette over the salad. Gently toss the fruit and lettuce together. Garnish with the papaya seeds. Serve immediately.

Serves 6

avocados and papayas

Avocados are one of the few fruits that do not ripen on the tree – they ripen after picking. It is better to buy a hard unripe avocado that hasn't been bruised by over-handling. To ripen it, place it on the counter and wait for a few days until it softens and ripens. To test for ripeness, place the avocado in the palm of your hand; if it yields to gentle pressure, it is ripe. If you need it to ripen more quickly, put the avocado in a paper bag with an apple and leave it in a cupboard. The apple releases a gas that should help ripen the avocado more quickly.

Papayas are available year-round. Look for yellowish to dark-orange fruit that has some give when pressed. Papayas should be ripened in a dark cupboard but not refrigerated, or they will lose their delicate flavour. Papaya seeds are edible and have a peppery, watercress-like taste. Use them as garnishes in salads.

eggplant tomato salad

Mix in sliced roasted red and green peppers, if desired.

1	eggplant, peeled	1
1 tsp	salt	5 mL
2 tbsp	vegetable oil	25 mL
3	tomatoes	3

spicy lemon vinaigrette

1 tsp	dried thyme	5 mL
1	clove garlic, minced	1
½ tsp	ground cumin	2 mL
pinch	cayenne pepper	pinch
1 tbsp	lemon juice	15 mL
½ cup	olive oil	125 mL

1 Cut the eggplant into slices ¼ inch (5 mm) thick and salt lightly. Leave for 15 minutes and pat dry.

2 Brush the eggplant slices with the oil. Place on a baking sheet. Broil until browned on 1 side, about 3 minutes. Turn over, oil the second side and broil until cooked through. Cool.

3 Cut the eggplant slices into strips and place in a large bowl. Cut the tomatoes into strips and toss with the eggplant.

4 In a small bowl, whisk together the vinaigrette ingredients. Pour over the eggplant and tomatoes and toss.

Serves 6

warm spring vegetable salad

If sugar snap peas are unavailable, substitute snow peas. Vegetables can be varied depending on availability and what you like, but remember to cut them all into even-sized chunks. Serve this salad warm with thin slices of French bread spread with homemade or commercial olive paste.

basil vinaigrette

	Grated rind and juice of 1 lemon	
2 tbsp	chopped fresh basil, or	25 mL
	2 tsp (10 mL) dried	
1 tsp	Dijon mustard	5 mL
½ cup	olive oil	125 mL
2	cloves garlic, slivered	2
2	medium zucchini, cut into ½-inch	2
	(1.25 cm) chunks	
4 oz	sugar snap peas	125 g
8 oz	asparagus, cut into	250 g
	2-inch (5 cm) pieces	
8	cherry tomatoes	8
	Salt and freshly	
	ground pepper to taste	
1	small head red leaf lettuce	1

1 To make the vinaigrette, in a large bowl, whisk together the lemon rind, lemon juice, basil and mustard. Slowly whisk in the olive oil. Reserve.

2 On high heat, bring a large pot of salted water to a boil. Add the slivered garlic and zucchini. Boil for 1 minute. Add the peas and asparagus. Boil for 1 minute longer, or until the vegetables are crisp-tender. Drain well, refresh with cold water and drain again.

3 Add the cooked vegetables and tomatoes to the bowl of vinaigrette. Toss the salad, adding salt and pepper as needed.

4 Place the lettuce leaves on a serving platter and pile the vegetables on top.

Serves 4

olive paste

Black olive paste can be purchased at gourmet food shops, or you can make your own by combining 6 oz (180 g) pitted black olives (preferably Greek or Italian) with 1 tsp (5 mL) dried thyme and 2 cloves garlic in the bowl of a food processor. Purée until coarsely chopped. With the machine running, add 3 tbsp (45 mL) olive oil through the feed tube. Purée until smooth.

Makes about ½ cup (125 mL)

field and flower salad

Use a variety of greens in this salad – arugula, lamb's lettuce (mache), endive, chicory, spinach, Boston lettuce and leaf lettuce. The sweet dressing pulls together all the tastes.

1	**head Boston lettuce**	1
1	**bunch arugula**	1
1 cup	**lamb's lettuce**	250 mL
1	**bunch watercress**	1
4	**sprigs chervil or Italian parsley**	4
1 tbsp	**chopped fresh tarragon**	15 mL
1	**small bunch primrose or nasturtium flowers**	1

honey vinaigrette

2 tbsp	**raspberry or white wine vinegar**	25 mL
2 tsp	**liquid honey**	10 mL
2 tbsp	**olive oil**	25 mL
2 tsp	**poppy seeds**	10 mL
	Salt and freshly ground pepper to taste	

1 Discard the arugula stalks. Tear the leaves into bite-sized pieces and place in a salad bowl.

2 Separate the lamb's lettuce leaves into clumps and remove the roots. Strip the watercress from its stalks. Add the lettuce and watercress to the salad bowl. Toss the chervil and tarragon with the lettuces and strew with the flowers.

3 To make the vinaigrette, whisk together the vinegar, honey, olive oil and poppy seeds in a small bowl. Season with salt and pepper. Pour over the salad and toss gently together. Serve immediately.

Serves 4 to 6

edible flowers

Salads can be enhanced by adding edible flowers, but make sure they are pesticide free. Buy them at a reliable greengrocer or pick them from your garden. Nasturtiums have a peppery taste and are high in vitamin C. Primroses are more delicate. Pansies have a tart flavour, and their purple heads look glorious mixed in with the green lettuces. The flowering tops of herbs look pretty and taste similar to the herb itself. Try chive tops, basil and tarragon flowers.

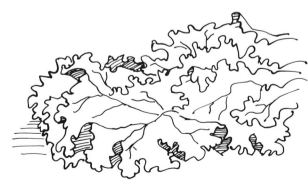

147

chicken and orange salad

The apple and curry mayonnaise lifts this salad out of its "everyday" classification. Serve it as a brunch dish or as a light salad supper. The mayonnaise is also delicious on poached salmon.

apple mayonnaise

1	apple	1
½ cup	chicken stock	125 mL
2 tsp	curry powder	10 mL
¾ cup	mayonnaise	175 mL
¼ cup	whipping cream	50 mL
1 tsp	grated orange rind	5 mL
1 tsp	dried tarragon	5 mL
	Salt and freshly ground pepper to taste	
6	single chicken breasts, poached, diced	6
2	seedless oranges	2
10 oz	fresh spinach	300 g
1 cup	seedless green grapes	250 mL

1 To make the mayonnaise, peel, core and dice the apple. In a small pot, combine the apple, chicken stock and curry powder. Cover and simmer over low heat until the apple has softened, about 2 minutes. Cool.

2 In a food processor, purée the apple mixture with the remaining mayonnaise ingredients until smooth. Reserve.

3 In a large bowl, fold the chicken into the mayonnaise. Peel the oranges, cutting away the white pith and membrane; separate into segments.

4 Line a serving platter with the spinach; pile chicken salad on top. Surround with the oranges and grapes.

Serves 6 as a main course

poaching chicken

If you are cooking chicken to use cold, poach it with the bones and skin still on. Bring a pot of water or chicken stock to the boil. Turn the heat to low and add chicken breasts. Simmer slowly (poach) for 35 to 40 minutes, or until the juices run clear. Cool the breasts in the liquid, then remove the bones and skin. The meat should be flavourful and juicy.

thai asparagus salad

This spectacular salad can be served as a first course or used as a buffet dish. Use ½ cup (125 mL) whipping cream blended with 2 tbsp (25 mL) desiccated coconut if you can't find coconut milk.

1½ lb	asparagus, peeled	750 g
1 tbsp	vegetable oil	15 mL
1	clove garlic, finely chopped	1
1 tsp	finely chopped fresh ginger	5 mL
1 tsp	dried chili flakes	5 mL
8 oz	shrimp, peeled	250 g
1 tbsp	soy sauce	15 mL

lime coconut dressing

	Grated rind and juice of 2 limes	
2 tbsp	vegetable oil	25 mL
1 tsp	dried basil	5 mL
1	clove garlic, minced	1
1 tsp	granulated sugar	5 mL
1 tbsp	fish sauce	15 mL
½ cup	coconut milk	125 mL
1 tsp	dried chili flakes	5 mL
1	head red leaf lettuce	1
4	green onions, thinly sliced	4
2 tbsp	chopped fresh coriander, optional	25 mL

1 Bring a large pot of water to a boil. Add the asparagus and cook until crisp-tender, about 3 minutes. Drain and run cold water over until cool. Reserve.

2 Heat the oil in a large skillet on high heat. Add the garlic, ginger and 1 tsp (5 mL) chili flakes. Stir-fry for 20 seconds.

3 Add the shrimp and stir-fry until pink and curled, about 2 minutes. Add the soy sauce and cool.

4 In a small bowl, whisk together the dressing ingredients. Reserve.

5 Cover a platter with red leaf lettuce. Fan the asparagus over top and scatter with the shrimp mixture. Pour the dressing over top and sprinkle on the green onions and coriander.

Serves 6

fennel and ham salad

When cooked, fennel is very mild, but when raw it is crisp and tangy. If prosciutto is unavailable, use smoked ham.

1	large bulb fennel	1
4 oz	prosciutto, chopped	125 g
1	bunch watercress, stems removed	1
8 oz	mushrooms, thinly sliced	250 g

tarragon vinaigrette

1/4 cup	lemon juice	50 mL
2 tsp	Dijon mustard	10 mL
1 tsp	dried tarragon	5 mL
1	small clove garlic, minced	1
1/2 cup	olive oil	125 mL
	Salt and freshly ground pepper to taste	

1 Trim the tops off the fennel bulb. Slice off the base and cut the fennel into quarters lengthwise. Slice the quarters thinly.
2 In a large bowl, combine the fennel with the prosciutto, watercress and mushrooms.
3 Whisk together the lemon juice, mustard, tarragon and garlic in a small bowl. Whisk in the olive oil. Season with the salt and pepper. Toss with the salad 30 minutes before serving to allow the flavours to mingle.

Serves 4

rice salad with ginger chili vinaigrette

Rice salads can be boring and bland, but this salad is full of fresh flavour and tangy crunch. Serve it as part of a buffet dinner or as a side dish at a barbecue.

ginger chili vinaigrette

	Grated rind and juice of 2 limes	
1 tsp	Dijon mustard	5 mL
1 tbsp	grated fresh ginger	15 mL
1 tsp	chili powder	5 mL
1/4 cup	sour cream	50 mL
1/2 tsp	granulated sugar	2 mL
1/4 cup	vegetable oil	50 mL
3 cups	cooked rice, warm	750 mL
1/2 cup	frozen or cooked peas	125 mL
1	small red pepper, finely chopped	1
1	small green pepper, finely chopped	1
8 oz	green beans, blanched and cut into 1/2-inch (1.25 cm) pieces	250 g
3	green onions, chopped	3
2	tomatoes, peeled, seeded and chopped	2

1 To make the vinaigrette, in a small bowl, whisk together the lime rind and juice, mustard, ginger, chili powder, sour cream and sugar. Slowly whisk in the oil.

150

2 In a large bowl, combine the warm rice with all the vegetables and the vinaigrette. Marinate for 30 minutes at room temperature or overnight in the refrigerator.

Serves 6

●●●●●●●●●●●●●●●

The secret to good rice or pasta salads is to toss them with the vinaigrette while they are still warm. Warm rice or pasta better absorbs the dressing and will have more flavour.

mint pesto pasta

Although pesto is traditionally made with basil, substituting mint leaves gives a fresh, exciting taste. Many gardens are overrun with mint in the summer, and this is an excellent way to use it up. If you make mint pesto for the freezer, omit the cheese, lemon juice and seasonings, which can be added after defrosting. Try this summery salad as part of a lunch buffet, or add cooked shrimp or chopped cooked chicken to the vegetables and serve as a main course.

1 lb	butterfly pasta (farfalle), or other short pasta	500 g

mint pesto

½ cup	pine nuts	125 mL
6	cloves garlic	6
3 cups	fresh mint leaves	750 mL
1 cup	olive oil	250 mL
½ cup	grated Parmesan cheese	125 mL
	Juice of 1 lemon	
	Salt and freshly ground pepper to taste	

1 cup	frozen peas, defrosted	250 mL
1	English cucumber, diced	1
4	green onions, sliced	4

1 Bring a large pot of salted water to a boil. Add the pasta and boil until *al dente*, about 10 minutes. Drain well and rinse with cold water. Drain again.

2 Meanwhile, in a food processor or blender, process the pine nuts, garlic and mint leaves until finely chopped.

3 With the machine running, pour the olive oil through the feed tube until combined. Add the cheese, lemon juice, salt and pepper.

4 Toss the pesto with the warm pasta. Mix in the peas, cucumber and green onions. Adjust the seasonings with salt and pepper and place on a serving platter.

Serves 6

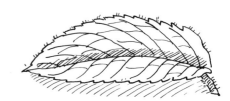

herb buttermilk dressing

A low-calorie dressing for any salad.

1 cup	buttermilk	250 mL
1 tbsp	finely chopped fresh dill	15 mL
1 tbsp	finely chopped parsley	15 mL
1 tsp	dried tarragon	5 mL
¼ tsp	Dijon mustard	1 mL
1	small clove garlic, minced	1
½ tsp	lemon juice	2 mL

1 Combine all the ingredients. Refrigerate for up to 1 week.
   Makes 1 cup (250 mL)

basic vinaigrette

This vinaigrette will dress up any salad, from simple leafy greens to more exotic vegetables and fruit. Make up the full amount and refrigerate until needed. It should keep for at least one month. Use about ⅓ cup (75 mL) vinaigrette for every 6 cups (1.5 L) greens.

1 tbsp	Dijon mustard	15 mL
¼ cup	wine vinegar	50 mL
¾ cup	olive or vegetable oil	175 mL

Salt and freshly ground pepper to taste

1 In a medium bowl, whisk together the mustard and vinegar.
2 Slowly whisk in the olive oil. The mixture should thicken. Season to taste with salt and pepper.
   Makes 1 cup (250 mL)

variations on the basic vinaigrette

- Garlic Vinaigrette: Add 1 minced clove garlic.
- Honey Mustard Vinaigrette: Add 1 tbsp (15 mL) liquid honey.
- Herb Vinaigrette: Add 2 tbsp (25 mL) chopped fresh herbs or 2 tsp (10 mL) dried herbs.
- Low-Cal Cheese Vinaigrette: Add ½ cup (125 mL) grated low-fat hard cheese.

QUICKBREADS & MUFFINS

chapter ten

*M*y family always appreciates homemade quickbreads. They taste wonderful, they are very homey, and I can control the amount of sugar and fat in them. Muffins, scones and biscuits are also quick to make and are excellent accompaniments to breakfasts, brunches and dinners. It takes no longer than five minutes to throw together a batch and usually about twenty minutes to bake.

153

tips

- The wet and dry ingredients for muffins should be lightly mixed together to ensure a moist texture. Over-mixing will make them dry.
- Scoop muffin batter into muffin cups with an ice-cream scoop to ensure even-sized muffins.
- Muffins, scones or biscuits can be made ahead and reheated at 350° F (180° C) for 5 minutes. The ingredients can also be measured the night before and mixed together just before baking.
- Only fill muffin cups two-thirds full to allow for rising. If you don't have enough batter to fill the pan, fill any empty cups with water before baking. This protects the cups and stops them from burning.

cheese scones

These cheesy scones are delicious in the morning with bacon and eggs. They also make sensational hamburger buns.

This recipe can also be made in a food processor, but be careful not to overprocess when adding the liquid; otherwise the scones will be tough. To prepare these ahead, combine the dry ingredients in advance, but don't add the milk until just before baking.

2½ cups	all-purpose flour	625 mL
4 tsp	baking powder	20 mL
2 tsp	dried mustard	10 mL
½ tsp	salt	2 mL
½ cup	butter, cut into cubes	125 mL
1½ cups	grated old Cheddar cheese (about 6 oz/180 g)	375 mL
1 cup	milk	250 mL
2 tbsp	whipping cream	25 mL

1 Preheat the oven to 425° F (210° C).
2 In a large bowl, combine the flour, baking powder, mustard and salt.
3 Cut the butter into the flour mixture with two knives or a pastry blender until the mixture resembles coarse breadcrumbs. Stir in the cheese.
4 Add the milk all at once and mix together with a fork until the dough begins to hold together. Turn the dough out onto a floured surface and knead gently 12 to 15

times until the dough forms a ball and is no longer sticky.

5 Roll out the dough until ¾ inch (2 cm) thick. Cut out 2-inch (5 cm) rounds with a cookie cutter.

6 Place the scones on ungreased baking sheets and brush with the cream. Bake for 15 to 18 minutes, or until pale gold.

Makes 12 scones

potato scones

A good recipe for using up leftover potatoes. Serve warm with butter or fry in bacon fat.

3	cooked peeled potatoes	3
¼ cup	butter, at room temperature	50 mL
	Salt and freshly	
	ground pepper to taste	
½ cup	all-purpose flour, approx.	125 mL

1 In a large bowl, mash the potatoes. Beat in the butter, salt and pepper. Stir in enough flour to make a soft dough.

2 Turn the dough out onto a floured board and knead. Form into 2-inch (5 cm) balls. Flatten into rounds and prick all over with a fork.

3 Dust a large skillet with flour. Cook the scones on medium-low heat until browned, about 2 minutes. Turn and cook the second side.

Makes about 12 scones

irish flat bread

This flat Irish potato bread tastes wonderful. Starch oozes from the potatoes to help bind the dough. Serve hot with lots of butter, or use to dip in gravy.

4	potatoes, peeled and grated (about 4 cups/1 L)	4
2 cups	mashed cooked potatoes	500 mL
3½ cups	all-purpose flour	875 mL
2 tsp	salt	10 mL
1 tsp	freshly ground pepper	5 mL
2 tbsp	baking powder	25 mL
½ cup	milk	125 mL
1	egg, beaten	1
2 tbsp	caraway seeds, optional	25 mL

1 Preheat the oven to 375° F (190° C).

2 In a large bowl, combine the grated and mashed potatoes, flour, salt and pepper. Stir in the baking powder and milk.

3 Knead the mixture on a floured board until smooth, about 5 minutes.

4 Divide the dough into four. Roll each piece out into a 6-inch (15 cm) circle. Place the rounds on buttered baking sheets, and brush generously with the beaten egg. Sprinkle with caraway seeds and mark a cross on each round to divide it into quarters.

5 Bake for 40 minutes, or until cooked through and lightly browned. Cool before cutting each loaf into quarters.

Makes 4 loaves

bacon cheddar muffins

A savoury muffin to serve at brunch or with soup for a light supper. You can also make these in small muffin cups (reduce the baking time to 10 to 15 minutes). Scoop out the centres of the baked mini muffins and fill with more grated Cheddar. Reheat at 350° F (180° C) for about five minutes, until the cheese melts, and serve as an hors d'oeuvre.

2 cups	all-purpose flour	500 mL
1 tbsp	baking powder	15 mL
1 tsp	salt	5 mL
2	eggs	2
1 cup	milk	250 mL
½ cup	butter, melted	125 mL
1 cup	grated old Cheddar cheese (about 4 oz/125 g)	250 mL
2 tbsp	chopped fresh dill	25 mL
6	strips bacon, cooked until crisp and crumbled	6
½ tsp	freshly ground pepper	2 mL

1 Preheat the oven to 400° F (200° C).
2 In a large bowl, combine the flour, baking powder and salt.
3 In a separate bowl, mix together the eggs, milk and melted butter.
4 Stir the liquid ingredients into the dry ingredients just until mixed. Stir in the cheese, dill, bacon and pepper.

5 Spoon the batter into 12 well-greased muffin cups and bake for 20 minutes, or until a toothpick inserted into the centre of a muffin comes out clean.
Makes 12 muffins

lemon yogourt muffins

A lemony muffin that goes well with tea.

1 cup	all-purpose flour	250 mL
1 cup	natural bran	250 mL
1 cup	rolled oats	250 mL
½ cup	granulated sugar	125 mL
2 tsp	baking powder	10 mL
1 tsp	baking soda	5 mL
½ tsp	salt	2 mL
1¼ cups	plain yogourt	300 mL
1	egg	1
¼ cup	lemon juice	50 mL
1	lemon, peeled and finely chopped (white pith removed)	1

syrup

¼ cup	granulated sugar	50 mL
	Grated rind and juice of ½ lemon	

1 Preheat the oven to 400° F (200° C).
2 In a large bowl, mix together the flour, bran, rolled oats, ½ cup (125 mL) sugar, baking powder, baking soda and salt.

3 In a separate bowl, mix together the yogourt, egg, ¼ cup (50 mL) lemon juice and chopped lemon.

4 Add the wet ingredients to the dry, mixing only until blended.

5 Fill 12 well-greased muffin cups two-thirds full. Bake for 20 minutes, or until a toothpick inserted into the centre of a muffin comes out clean.

6 Meanwhile, prepare the syrup. Put ¼ cup (50 mL) sugar and the lemon rind and juice in a small pot. Bring to a boil and reserve.

7 When the muffins are baked, prick all over with a toothpick. Do not remove them from the pan until cooked. Brush the warm syrup on the hot muffins.

Makes 12 muffins

fresh ginger lime bran muffins

This sophisticated muffin was recently voted the best in my cooking school classes. It is moist, gingery and definitely different.

¼ cup	grated fresh ginger	50 mL
	(about one 2½-inch/6.25 cm piece)	
¾ cup	granulated sugar	175 mL
	Grated rind and juice of 1 lime	

½ cup	butter, at room temperature	125 mL
2	eggs	2
1 cup	buttermilk	250 mL
1 cup	all-purpose flour	250 mL
1¾ cups	natural bran	425 mL
½ tsp	salt	2 mL
¾ tsp	baking soda	4 mL

1 Preheat the oven to 375° F (190° C).

2 Put the ginger and ¼ cup (50 mL) sugar in a small pot. Add the lime rind and juice. Cook over medium heat, stirring, until the sugar has melted and the mixture is hot. Remove from the heat and set aside.

3 In a large bowl, beat the butter with the remaining ½ cup (125 mL) sugar until smooth. Add the eggs and beat well. Add the buttermilk and mix until blended.

4 In a separate bowl, combine the flour, bran, salt and baking soda. Add to the wet ingredients and beat until smooth. Add the ginger/lime mixture and mix until blended.

5 Spoon the batter into 12 well-greased muffin cups. Bake for 20 to 25 minutes, or until a toothpick comes out clean when inserted into the centre of a muffin.

Makes 12 muffins

peanut butter banana muffins

A real kid-pleaser and a healthy snack, this moist muffin is perfect for peanut butter fans.

2 cups	all-purpose flour	500 mL
½ cup	lightly packed brown sugar	125 mL
1 tbsp	baking powder	15 mL
¼ tsp	salt	1 mL
½ cup	peanut butter	125 mL
2 tbsp	vegetable oil	25 mL
2	eggs	2
¾ cup	milk	175 mL
2	ripe bananas, mashed	2

1 Preheat the oven to 375° F (190° C).
2 In a large bowl, mix together the flour, brown sugar, baking powder and salt.
3 In a separate bowl, beat together the peanut butter, oil, eggs, milk and bananas.
4 Stir the wet ingredients into the dry ingredients just until moistened.
5 Spoon the batter into 12 well-greased muffin cups. Bake for 20 to 25 minutes, or until a toothpick inserted in the centre of a muffin comes out clean.
   Makes 12 muffins

strawberry rhubarb muffins

The sweetness of the strawberries contrasts with the tart rhubarb. This is an excellent dessert-type muffin.

1¾ cups	all-purpose flour	425 mL
½ cup	granulated sugar	125 mL
2 tsp	baking powder	10 mL
½ tsp	salt	2 mL
2 tsp	grated orange rind	10 mL
1	egg	1
¾ cup	milk	175 mL
⅓ cup	vegetable oil	75 mL
1 cup	finely chopped rhubarb	250 mL
½ cup	sliced strawberries	125 mL
Granulated sugar for dusting		

1 Preheat the oven to 400° F (200° C).
2 In a large bowl, combine the flour, sugar, baking powder, salt and orange rind.
3 In a separate bowl, beat together the egg, milk and oil.
4 Stir the wet ingredients into the dry ingredients. Gently stir in the rhubarb and strawberries. Do not overmix.
5 Fill 12 well-greased muffin cups two-thirds full with the batter. Sprinkle the muffin tops lightly with sugar.

6 Bake for 20 to 25 minutes, or until a toothpick inserted in the centre of a muffin comes out clean.

Makes 12 muffins

buttermilk biscuits

Serve these biscuits with Southern Fried Chicken (see page 66) or pork chops as a starch alternative. When baking, remember to make sure the biscuits touch each other. This gives them a softer outside crust.

2 cups	all-purpose flour	500 mL
2 tsp	baking powder	10 mL
½ tsp	baking soda	2 mL
1 tsp	granulated sugar	5 mL
¾ tsp	salt	4 mL
⅔ cup	cold vegetable shortening or butter, cut into cubes	150 mL
¾ cup	buttermilk	175 mL

glaze

1 tbsp	buttermilk	15 mL

1 Preheat the oven to 400° F (200° C).
2 In a large bowl, stir together the flour, baking powder, baking soda, sugar and salt.

3 Using two knives or a pastry blender, cut in the shortening or butter until the mixture resembles coarse crumbs.
4 Pour in ¾ cup (175 mL) buttermilk and stir together with your fingers or a fork until all the ingredients are moistened. The mixture should be slightly sticky. Gently shape into a ball.
5 On a floured board, knead the dough 5 or 6 times. Pat or roll into a rectangle about ½ inch (1.25 cm) thick. With a 2-inch cookie cutter, cut the dough into rounds and place in a greased 9-inch (23 cm) square baking pan with the sides of the biscuits touching.
6 Brush the biscuits with the remaining 1 tbsp (15 mL) buttermilk and bake for 15 to 18 minutes, or until golden-brown.

Makes 16 biscuits

spoonbread

Spoonbread is more like a pudding than a firm cornbread. It is spooned out at the table and served with fried or grilled chicken, pork chops or spareribs. It is terrific with dishes that have sauces because the bread absorbs the gravy, but I like it slathered with butter and eaten for breakfast. For an even lighter spoonbread, separate the eggs and beat the yolks into the batter. Beat the egg whites until stiff and fold in just before baking. You can also add ¼ cup (50 mL) chopped green onion and/or chopped red pepper for colour and crunch, and chopped chilies to taste.

1½ cups	water	375 mL
1 cup	yellow cornmeal	250 mL
½ cup	butter, at room temperature	125 mL
1 tsp	salt	5 mL
1 tsp	granulated sugar	5 mL
3	eggs, slightly beaten	3
1 cup	milk	250 mL
2 tsp	baking powder	10 mL

1 Preheat the oven to 375° F (190° C).
2 In a large pot, bring the water to a boil on high heat. Whisk in the cornmeal in a steady stream.
3 Reduce the heat to medium. Stir in the butter, salt and sugar and simmer for 5 minutes, stirring constantly. Cool slightly.
4 Beat the eggs into the cornmeal mixture, then beat in the milk and baking powder.

5 Spoon the batter into a buttered 8-inch (20 cm) square baking dish or a cast-iron skillet. Bake for 40 minutes, or until a toothpick inserted in the centre comes out clean.
Serves 6

cornmeal

Cornmeal is sold as white, yellow or stoneground. White cornmeal comes from white varieties of corn; yellow cornmeal from yellow varieties. Yellow cornmeal has a slightly stronger cornmeal taste. Stoneground cornmeal has a certain percentage of corn bran in it. Store cornmeal in the cupboard.

160

wafer biscuits

An easy, crisp cracker to serve with soup, dips and salads.

2½ cups	all-purpose flour	625 mL
2 tbsp	granulated sugar	25 mL
½ tsp	salt	2 mL
½ tsp	baking soda	2 mL
½ cup	butter, cut into cubes	125 mL
1 cup	plain yogourt	250 mL
¼ cup	grated Parmesan cheese	50 mL

1 In a food processor or by hand, combine the flour, sugar, salt and baking soda. Cut in the butter until the mixture resembles coarse crumbs.
2 Add the yogourt and blend until the mixture forms a soft dough. Wrap in waxed paper and chill for 15 minutes.
3 Preheat the oven to 400° F (200° C).
4 Break off marble-sized pieces of dough and roll until ⅛ inch (3 mm) thick.
5 Transfer to an ungreased baking sheet and sprinkle with cheese. Bake for 5 minutes. Turn off the oven and leave until crisp, about 30 minutes.
Makes 30 biscuits

cheese rounds

These cheese biscuits can be made up to three days ahead. Serve at room temperature or reheat at 300° F (150° C) for five minutes. Serve them as hors d'oeuvres or alongside a soup or salad.

You can also shape the dough into pretzels or sticks. Paint them with beaten egg white and sprinkle with sesame seeds before baking, to enhance the pretzel-like look.

½ cup	butter, at room temperature	125 mL
2½ cups	grated old Cheddar cheese (about 10 oz/300 g)	625 mL
2 tbsp	Dijon mustard	25 mL
1¼ cups	all-purpose flour	300 mL
1 tsp	salt	5 mL
¼ tsp	cayenne pepper	1 mL

1 Preheat the oven to 375° F (190° C).
2 In a food processor or by hand, cream the butter until fluffy. Add the cheese and mustard and process until well combined.
3 In a medium bowl, combine the flour, salt and cayenne. Add to the cheese mixture and combine just until the dough holds together. Do not over-mix.
4 Divide the dough into 2 portions and shape into cylinders about 2 inches (5 cm) in diameter. Cut slices about ¼ inch (5 mm) thick and place on ungreased baking sheets, about 2 inches (5 cm) apart. Bake for 12 to 15 minutes, or until pale gold.
Makes about 24 rounds

homemade apricot marmalade

A quick homemade apricot preserve with a subtle orange background. Any leftover preserve should keep for one month in the refrigerator (if it doesn't disappear first on your morning toast or muffin).

In a heavy pot, place 2 cups (500 mL) chopped dried apricots, the grated rind of 2 oranges, 1 cup (250 mL) dry white wine, 1 cup (250 mL) water and 2 tbsp (25 mL) granulated sugar. Simmer together, covered, for 30 minutes, stirring occasionally, until the apricots are very soft. Cool and place in clean, dry jars. Makes about three 8-oz (250 g) jars. Keep refrigerated.

quick tips for leftover muffins

■ To make a quick bread pudding, cut two or three sweet muffins into slices and place in a baking dish. Make a custard mixture of 2 eggs and ⅔ cup (150 mL) milk. Sweeten with sugar to taste and, if desired, add a handful of raisins, chopped dried fruit or chopped fresh fruit. Pour the mixture over the muffins and bake at 325° F (160° C) for 20 to 40 minutes, or until a knife inserted into the centre of the pudding comes out clean.

■ Crumble leftover biscuits or soda bread and use in your favourite stuffing for chicken or turkey.

■ Break up sweet muffins and combine with melted butter until crumbly. Use as a topping for fruit crisps.

■ Cut sweet muffins into slices and spread with raspberry jam. Layer in a dish with custard. Soak well with sherry and top with whipped cream for a spectacular trifle.

■ Sauté crumbled sweet muffins in butter until coated. Layer with applesauce in a buttered baking dish. Let sit for a few hours in the refrigerator. Serve with ice cream.

chapter eleven

FRUIT DESSERTS & QUICK CONFECTIONS

*F*or the person in a hurry, making desserts is probably the
hardest part of preparing a meal. The thought of whipping up
a last-minute cake or pie is out of the question, but there are many
wonderful desserts that can be put together with time to spare.
You can also dress up store-bought items easily. What's better
than a fabulous ice cream served with homemade caramel sauce,
or a plate of fresh sliced fruit accompanied by a piece of ripe,
mellow Brie?

163

tips

- Fruit is the mainstay of faster desserts. It is best to buy fruit in season because out-of-season berries or tree fruit often appear to be bred for looks alone, and have little taste.
- Fruit salads are one of the quickest ways to prepare fresh fruit. They can be served with the simplest marinating sauce of plain white wine, or a more complicated sauce of jam, liqueurs and flavourings.
- Although baking may not be considered something in the lexicon of the quick cook, there are a number of easy squares that can be assembled and baked in less than forty minutes.
- Presentation can make the difference between an ordinary dessert and something special. Try serving fools or fruits in large wine glasses, or garnish fresh fruit with a sprig of mint and some grated lemon rind.
- Make squares in advance and keep them on hand stored in a cookie tin. They can be served as a snack with a cup of coffee, or they can be dressed up with a scoop of whipped cream or ice cream and served for dessert.

apple ginger crisp

This luscious crisp takes no time to assemble because the topping is made from ginger cookies. Use shortbread cookies if ginger is not to your taste. Try a mixture of rhubarb and strawberries instead of the apples. Serve warm with ice cream or custard.

5	apples	5
¼ cup	brown sugar	50 mL
	Juice of ½ lemon	
2 tbsp	butter	25 mL

topping

1½ cups	crushed ginger cookies	375 mL
2 tbsp	brown sugar	25 mL
½ cup	butter, at room temperature	125 mL

1 Preheat the oven to 375° F (190° C).
2 Peel, core and thinly slice the apples. In a large bowl, combine the apples, ¼ cup (50 mL) sugar and lemon juice.
3 Spoon the filling into a buttered 11 x 7-inch (2 L) baking dish. Dot with the butter.
4 In a medium bowl, combine the topping ingredients. Scatter over the apple mixture.
5 Bake for 35 minutes, or until the juices bubble up.

Serves 6

baked apples

A fast low-cal baked apple that cooks while you prepare the rest of dinner.

4	apples	4
2 tbsp	raisins	25 mL
	Ground cinnamon	
	and grated nutmeg to taste	
1 tbsp	brown sugar	15 mL
1 cup	orange juice	250 mL

1 Preheat the oven to 350° F (180° C).
2 Core the apples and peel off the skin around the stem. Place in an 8-inch (2 L) square baking dish.
3 In a small bowl, combine the raisins, cinnamon, nutmeg and sugar.
4 Fill the centres of the apples with the raisin mixture. Pour the orange juice over the apples.
5 Bake for 45 minutes, basting occasionally, until the apples are soft.
    Serves 4

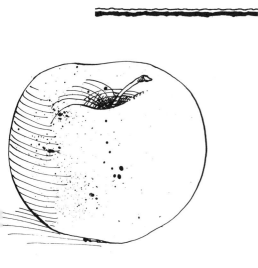

apple cranberry compote

To mellow the tartness of the cranberries, the sugar syrup has to be sweet. This is a good Christmas dessert after a heavy meal. You can serve the compote warm or cold. It should keep for two weeks, refrigerated.

½ cup	butter	125 mL
1 cup	granulated sugar	250 mL
2	tart green apples, peeled	2
	and sliced	
1 cup	fresh or frozen cranberries	250 mL
2 cups	vanilla ice cream	500 mL
1 tsp	ground cinnamon	5 mL

1 Combine the butter and sugar in a large skillet on medium-high heat. Bring to a boil and boil for 1 minute.
2 Add the apple slices and cranberries. Lower the heat and simmer until the apples are tender and the cranberries just begin to pop, about 10 minutes.
3 To serve, spoon the ice cream into dishes and sprinkle with cinnamon. Top with the warm cranberry apple compote.
    Serves 4

layered berry salad

Use whichever fresh berries are available, and try to make the salad in a glass bowl, because the layers of fruit look very pretty. The recipe can be doubled or tripled with ease. The compote should keep for up to three days in the refrigerator. Serve it with whipped cream, garnished with sprigs of fresh mint.

8 oz	cherries, pitted	250 g
2 cups	blueberries	500 mL
2 cups	strawberries, hulled and halved	500 mL
1 cup	raspberries	250 mL

syrup

¼ cup	red currant jelly	50 mL
¼ cup	sherry	50 mL
2 tsp	grated orange rind	10 mL
2 tsp	grated fresh ginger	10 mL

1 Layer the fruit in a glass bowl.
2 To make the syrup, in a small pot, bring the jelly, sherry, orange rind and ginger to a boil; remove from the heat and cool.
3 Pour the syrup over the fruit.
Serves 4 to 6

When buying berries in a carton, look at the bottom of the carton. If it is stained with juice, the berries are likely overripe or squashed.

fruit dip for berries

Use cherries and strawberries because they are the easiest to handle as dippers. You can include raspberries, blueberries and currants if you provide individual bowls.

dip

½ cup	ground almonds	125 mL
1 cup	plain yogourt	250 mL
2 tbsp	liquid honey	25 mL
1 tsp	almond extract	5 mL
1 tbsp	finely chopped candied ginger	15 mL
10 cups	mixed berries	2.5 L

1 Place the almonds in a food processor and process until pasty. Add the yogourt, honey, almond extract and ginger and combine until mixed. Place in a serving bowl.
2 Arrange the fruit on a large platter, placing the dip in the centre. If using individual bowls, spoon the dip over the fruit.
Serves 8

cherry clafouti

Clafouti is similar to an oven-cooked crêpe. It can be made with any fruit. Plum, peach or blueberry clafouti are also particularly good. If you do not feel like pitting the cherries, you can use them whole.

¼ cup	all-purpose flour	50 mL
⅓ cup	granulated sugar	75 mL
3	eggs	3
1	egg yolk	1
1¾ cups	milk	425 mL
1 tsp	vanilla extract	5 mL
1 lb	cherries, pitted	500 g

1 In a large bowl, mix together the flour and sugar.

2 In a small bowl, whisk together the eggs, egg yolk, milk and vanilla.

3 Add the wet ingredients to the dry and combine. Let stand for 15 minutes.

4 Preheat the oven to 400° F (200° C).

5 Butter an 8-inch (2 L) square baking dish. Pour a film of batter over the bottom. Scatter the cherries on top. Pour over the remaining batter.

6 Bake for 30 to 40 minutes, or until puffed.

Serves 4 to 6

fresh cherries with sour cream dip

If you don't have a cherry pitter, serve the cherries with the stems attached. Other fruits can be added to the platter, if desired.

½ cup	sour cream	125 mL
2 tbsp	brown sugar	25 mL
1 lb	fresh Bing cherries	500 g
	Fresh mint leaves	

1 Combine the sour cream and brown sugar in a small attractive bowl. Place the bowl in the centre of a platter and pile the cherries around.

2 Garnish the dip with mint leaves and scatter mint leaves over the cherries.

Serves 4

cherries with goat cheese

Cherries seem to bring out the best in strongly flavoured goat cheese. If goat cheese is unavailable, use Brie.

1 lb	cherries	500 g
4 oz	goat cheese	125 g
	Fresh mint leaves	

1 Arrange the fruit and cheese on 4 individual serving plates. Refrigerate until needed.
2 When ready to serve, garnish with mint.
Serves 4

cherries

The best cherries are Bings – the darkest ones are usually the juiciest. Look for plump shiny fruit with the stems attached. If the stems have fallen off, the fruit isn't at its freshest.

To pit cherries easily, use a cherry pitter – a gadget that punches through the cherry and removes the stone. If you do not have a pitter, cut the cherry in half and lever out the pit. With tart red cherries, press the whole cherry gently; the pit should pop out.

mango fool

Fools are fruit-streaked cream desserts that are easy to make and delightful to eat. You can use any soft-textured ripe fruit instead of mangoes.

2	mangoes, peeled	2
¼ cup	granulated sugar, or to taste	50 mL
1 cup	whipping cream	250 mL

1 Thinly slice half a mango and reserve for the garnish.
2 Combine the remaining mangoes and sugar in a food processor or blender. Purée until smooth. Taste and add more sugar if necessary.
3 In a large bowl, whip the cream until it holds its shape. Fold in the mango purée. Refrigerate until needed. Serve in wine glasses, garnished with the reserved slices of mango.
Serves 4

figs

Figs are the most luscious of fruits. They can be black or green, depending on the variety. Look for plump, sweet-smelling figs that give a little when pressed. Their exotic look dresses up a cheese or fruit tray.

168

figs with mascarpone

Mascarpone has a slightly tart, but not sour, taste. If you can't find it and don't want to make your own, the best substitute is ricotta cheese flavoured with a little grated lemon rind.

8	figs	8
1 cup	mascarpone cheese	250 mL
2 tbsp	icing sugar	25 mL
¼ cup	orange liqueur	50 mL

1 Quarter each fig, without slicing completely through, so it will open like a flower.
2 In a small bowl, combine the mascarpone, sugar and 2 tbsp (25 mL) orange liqueur. Mound in centre of 4 plates, placing two figs on either side. Dribble the remaining orange liqueur over the figs.
Serves 4

homemade mascarpone

Although it is available at better cheese stores and Italian groceries, mascarpone is easy to make.

In a small pot, combine 1 cup (250 mL) whipping cream with ½ tsp

(2 mL) tartaric acid and heat to a simmer. Remove from the heat and let sit for 24 hours at room temperature (the mixture should thicken). Refrigerate for up to one week.

ambrosia

An old Southern dessert that is perfect in the winter when oranges and pineapples are plentiful. This is an ideal dessert to make a day ahead because the longer it stands, the more juice leaks out from the fruit and the better it tastes. (Southerners would pour ½ cup/125 mL sherry over this dessert before serving.)

4	oranges	4
1	pineapple	1
1 cup	desiccated coconut	250 mL
½ cup	icing sugar	125 mL

1 Peel the oranges, making sure you remove all the white pith and skin. Slice into rounds.
2 Peel the pineapple and slice it into quarters. Remove the core and cut the flesh into chunks.
3 Layer the oranges and pineapple in a serving bowl, sprinkling each layer with coconut and icing sugar.
Serves 6

sliced peaches with champagne bellinis

Bellinis are a delectable Italian Champagne tipple, first served in the famous Harry's Bar in Venice. Serve the bellinis in Champagne flutes, to be sipped while you are eating the succulent peaches.

This drink/dessert combination is the perfect ending to a barbecue meal. For an even simpler version, pop a whole peeled and sliced peach into a large balloon glass and top with Champagne. Drink the Champagne, then nibble on the peach.

2 tbsp	granulated sugar	25 mL
2 tbsp	lemon juice	25 mL
5	ripe peaches, peeled and sliced	5
1	bottle Champagne	1

1 Sprinkle the sugar and lemon juice on 4 peaches and arrange slices decoratively on 4 serving plates.

2 To prepare the bellinis, peel the remaining peach and purée in a food processor or blender. Place 1 tbsp (15 mL) purée in each of 4 Champagne flutes. Top up with the Champagne.

3 Serve the sliced peaches and bellinis together.

Serves 4

schnapped peaches

This simple peach dessert can be made up to three hours ahead. Or let the peaches marinate in the schnapps overnight.

4	ripe peaches, peeled	4
¼ cup	peach schnapps	50 mL
½ cup	whipping cream	125 mL
	Grated rind and juice of 1 orange	

1 Thinly slice the peaches and place in a bowl.

2 Pour the peach schnapps over the peaches and marinate at room temperature for 15 minutes.

3 In a separate bowl, whip the cream until it holds its shape. Beat in the orange rind and juice.

4 Pile the peaches into individual glass dishes, pouring any remaining juices over them. Spoon on the whipped cream.

Serves 4

low-cal peach yogourt

Add ¼ cup (50 mL) fresh peach purée to plain non-fat or low-fat yogourt for a snack or dessert. It has approximately 120 calories per 8 oz (250 g) – 50 percent fewer calories than most commercial peach yogourts.

fresh peach raspberry chocolate tart

This uncooked pie works equally well with blueberries or any other fresh fruit. The secret is to cook half the fruit with the cornstarch and then fold in the remainder.

1½ cups	chocolate wafers, crushed (about 30 wafers)	375 mL
¼ cup	icing sugar	50 mL
⅓ cup	butter, melted	75 mL

filling

2 cups	frozen raspberries, thawed,	500 mL
⅓ cup	granulated sugar	75 mL
3 tbsp	lemon juice	45 mL
2 tbsp	cornstarch	25 mL
4	fresh peaches, peeled and thinly sliced	4

1 Combine the crushed wafers, icing sugar and butter in a medium bowl and mix well.

2 Gently press the wafer mixture into a 9-inch (23 cm) tart pan. Chill until ready to fill.

3 To make the filling, purée the raspberries in a blender or food processor.

4 Combine the raspberries, sugar, lemon juice and cornstarch in a medium pot. Stir over medium-high heat for 4 minutes, or until very thick.

5 Stir the peaches into the raspberry purée. Pour into the crust and chill until firm, about 1 hour.

Serves 8

peaches

The best peaches for eating and cooking are freestone – the flesh does not adhere to the pit, but comes away easily. Clingstone peaches (the flesh adheres to the pit) are used for processing or canning.

To peel peaches easily, bring a pot of water to a boil, drop in the peaches and leave for 30 seconds. Drain. The skins should slip right off.

buttered pears with cambozola

If Comice pears are available, they are wonderful for eating and cooking, but if not, use Anjou. If the pears are at the height of their season, don't precook them; just heat the butter and sugar together, pour over the pears and continue with the recipe.

If you can't find Cambozola, sprinkle cubes of Camembert over the pears and grate about 2 tbsp (25 mL) Danish blue over top.

2 tbsp	butter	25 mL
1 tbsp	brown sugar	15 mL
2	pears, peeled, cored and sliced	2
2 oz	Cambozola cheese	60 g

1 Preheat the oven to 400° F (200° C).
2 In a large skillet on medium heat, melt the butter and sugar.
3 Add the pears and sauté until slightly softened, about 5 minutes.
4 Place the pears in a buttered ovenproof gratin dish and pour the syrup over top.
5 Cut the Cambozola into cubes and scatter over the pears. Bake for 5 minutes, or until the cheese melts. Serve hot.
Serves 4

cambozola

Cambozola cheese is made in Germany; it is a combination of Camembert and Gorgonzola. It is quite creamy and mild, but the riper the cheese, the stronger the flavour. It's a cheese that people who don't like strong-flavoured blue cheeses usually enjoy.

rhubarb crisp

Spoon this spicy rhubarb filling over praline ice cream for a real treat.

2 lb	rhubarb	1 kg
½ cup	brown sugar	125 mL
½ tsp	ground ginger	2 mL
½ tsp	ground cinnamon	2 mL
½ tsp	grated nutmeg	2 mL
2 tbsp	grated orange rind	25 mL
2 tbsp	butter	25 mL

topping

½ cup	brown sugar	125 mL
½ cup	all-purpose flour	125 mL
¾ cup	granola	175 mL
½ cup	butter, cut into cubes	125 mL

1 Cut the rhubarb into 2-inch (5 cm) pieces.

2 In a large pot, mix together the rhubarb, ½ cup (125 mL) sugar, ginger, cinnamon, nutmeg, orange rind and 2 tbsp (25 mL) butter. Cook on medium heat, uncovered, for 10 minutes, or until the rhubarb softens.

3 Preheat the oven to 375° F (190° C).

4 To make the topping, mix ½ cup (125 mL) sugar with the flour and granola in a bowl. Cut in the butter with a pastry blender or your fingers until the mixture resembles small peas. Alternatively, combine the topping ingredients in a food processor and blend until crumbly (do not overprocess).

5 Place the softened rhubarb in a greased 11 x 7-inch (2 L) baking dish. Press on the topping, making sure the whole surface is covered.

6 Bake for 20 to 25 minutes, or until the top is browned and the rhubarb is syrupy.

Serves 4 to 6

rhubarb

Rhubarb varies in sweetness depending on whether it is garden grown or hothouse forced. Hothouse rhubarb is usually sweeter, but garden rhubarb has more taste. Always sweeten rhubarb to taste.

rhubarb fool

A delightful light recipe to follow any heavy meal. Taste the rhubarb before adding the whipping cream in case it needs extra sugar. A spoonful of chopped candied ginger can be added to the rhubarb before cooking for a flavour change.

Fools, if left sitting for more than a few hours, will separate. Stir together to combine again.

2 lb	rhubarb	1 kg
½ cup	brown sugar	125 mL
2 tbsp	water	25 mL
1 tbsp	grated orange rind	15 mL
1 cup	whipping cream	250 mL

1 Cut the rhubarb into 2-inch (2.5 cm) lengths.

2 In a medium pot, combine the rhubarb, sugar, water and grated orange rind. Cook together on low heat until the rhubarb softens, about 10 minutes. Cool and drain off the liquid, reserving ¼ cup (50 mL) juice.

3 Place the rhubarb and reserved juice in a food processor or blender and purée until smooth.

4 In a large bowl, whip the cream until it holds its shape.

5 Fold the rhubarb purée into the cream. Spoon into glass dishes and chill before serving.

Serves 4

strawberries with raspberry sauce

The raspberry sauce also goes well with fresh peaches or chocolate cake. Garnish the dessert with whipped cream or ice cream, if desired.

4 cups	fresh strawberries	1 L
2 tbsp	icing sugar	25 mL
¼ cup	orange liqueur	50 mL

raspberry sauce

1	10-oz (300 g) package frozen raspberries in syrup	1
1 tbsp	lemon juice	15 mL

1 Hull the strawberries, leaving them whole. Place in a bowl and sprinkle with the icing sugar and liqueur.
2 To make the sauce, slightly defrost the raspberries, then place in a food processor or blender and purée until smooth. Mix in the lemon juice.
3 Strain the sauce through a sieve into a bowl to remove the seeds.
4 To serve, place a film of raspberry sauce on each plate and spoon the strawberries on top.
Serves 4

If you overwhip your cream and it starts to turn to butter, stir in a few more spoonfuls of cream to soften it.

strawberry chantilly

This dessert can be elegant or casual, depending on how you present it. For an elegant presentation, serve in balloon wine glasses. For a more casual effect, pile into a bowl and scoop out onto serving dishes.

4 cups	fresh strawberries	1 L
2 tbsp	orange liqueur	25 mL
⅔ cup	whipping cream	125 mL
2 tbsp	granulated sugar	25 mL
½ cup	sour cream	125 mL

1 Hull the strawberries. Place all but 6 strawberries in a food processor or blender and purée with the liqueur.
2 In a large bowl, whip the cream with the sugar until the mixture holds its shape. Fold in the sour cream. Fold in the purée.
3 Slice the reserved strawberries and use as a garnish.
Serves 4 to 6

watermelon and strawberry cream

If yellow watermelon is available, use it for colour contrast. If you don't have kirsch, use any orange liqueur.

½	watermelon	½
2 cups	strawberries, hulled	500 mL
1 cup	whipping cream	250 mL
2 tbsp	kirsch	25 mL

1 Peel and cube the watermelon and divide among 4 serving plates.
2 In a food processor, purée the strawberries.
3 In a large bowl, whip the cream until it holds its shape. Flavour with the kirsch. Fold in the strawberry purée and pile on top of the watermelon.
Serves 4

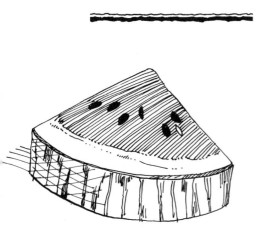

lemon curd

Lemon curd can be used to fill tartlet shells, as a cookie sandwich filling or instead of custard in pie shells. It is also used as a spread for scones and toast. Lemon curd should keep for up to one month in a refrigerator. Use lime juice in place of lemon for a flavour twist.

1 cup	granulated sugar	250 mL
½ cup	butter	125 mL
2 tbsp	grated lemon rind	25 mL
¼ cup	lemon juice	50 mL
3	eggs, well beaten	3

1 Combine all the ingredients in a heavy pot. Stir gently over low heat until the mixture is thick and coats the back of the spoon, 10 to 15 minutes. Do not let the mixture boil, or it will curdle.
2 Remove from the heat. Place plastic wrap directly on top of the mixture and allow to cool (this should stop the mixture from forming a skin). Refrigerate until needed.
Makes about 2 cups (500 mL)

lemon posset

Originally an old English dish served from Elizabethan times on, this simple and refreshing dessert is a fine end to a heavy meal. It can be made up to three hours ahead and refrigerated until serving.

Grated rind and juice of 2 lemons		
½ cup	granulated sugar	125 mL
2 cups	whipping cream	500 mL
½ cup	dry sherry	125 mL

1 In a large bowl, combine the lemon rind and juice with the sugar. Add the cream and whip until the mixture thickens and holds its shape.

2 Fold in the sherry. Serve the posset in glasses, garnished with some extra grated lemon rind or a few blueberries.

Serves 4

juicing lemons

Choose lemons that are heavy for their size. To get the most juice from them, microwave at high power (100%) for 20 seconds, or roll heavily on the counter before cutting.

derby squares

These racy squares, the kind that people take to tailgate picnics at the Kentucky Derby, are mouth-watering and easily portable. They are a cross between a butter tart and pecan pie.

base

1 cup	all-purpose flour	250 mL
2 tbsp	granulated sugar	25 mL
½ cup	softened butter	125 mL

filling

3	eggs	3
½ cup	brown sugar	125 mL
2 tbsp	all-purpose flour	25 mL
¼ cup	melted butter	50 mL
1 cup	corn syrup	250 mL
1 tbsp	vinegar	15 mL
1 tsp	vanilla	5 mL
	Pinch salt	
1 cup	pecans, halved	250 mL
1 cup	chopped chocolate or chocolate chips	250 mL

1 Preheat oven to 350 F (180 C). Grease an 8-inch (2 L) square cake pan.

2 Combine flour, sugar and butter in a food processor and process until mixture is crumbly. Press into prepared pan. Bake for 15 minutes, or until slightly coloured. Remove from oven.

3 Beat eggs until foamy. Beat in brown sugar and flour. Stir in melted butter, corn syrup, vinegar, vanilla, salt, pecans and chocolate.

4 Pour into partially baked base and bake for 30 to 40 minutes, or until golden brown on top and a toothpick comes out clean.

5 Cool and cut into rectangles.
Makes about 20 bars

chocolate chip squares

These easy-to-make squares freeze well and are perfect for bag lunches.

base

⅓ cup	granulated sugar	75 mL
1 cup	all-purpose flour	250 mL
½ cup	butter, cut into cubes	125 mL

topping

6 oz	bittersweet chocolate, cut into chunks, or semi-sweet chocolate chips	180 g
¾ cup	brown sugar	175 mL
2	eggs	2
2 tbsp	all-purpose flour	25 mL
1 tsp	baking powder	5 mL
½ cup	desiccated coconut	125 mL
1 tsp	vanilla extract	5 mL
½ cup	chopped walnuts	125 mL

1 Preheat the oven to 350° F (180° C).

2 To make the base, in a medium bowl, combine the granulated sugar and 1 cup (250 mL) flour. Using a pastry blender or two knives, cut in the butter until the mixture resembles coarse breadcrumbs. Press the mixture into a greased 8-inch (2 L) square cake pan. Bake for 20 minutes.

3 Remove the pan from the oven and sprinkle base with chocolate chunks.

4 Combine the remaining ingredients in a bowl. Spread over the chocolate chunks. Bake for 20 to 30 minutes, or until the top is golden-brown (the squares should still be soft). Cool in the pan before cutting into squares.

Makes 16 2-inch (5 cm) squares

sabayon

Sabayon is a frothy warm custard made with white wine or champagne. Generally it is spooned over cooked or uncooked fruits. Unless it is served cold, sabayon has to be made just before serving.

warm sabayon

6	**egg yolks**	6
1/3 cup	**sugar**	75 mL
1 cup	**white wine**	250 mL
2 tbsp	**orange liqueur**	25 mL
	Mixture of berries, exotic fruits	
	or poached pears	

1 Place a large metal bowl over a pot of water simmering on medium heat. Add egg yolks, sugar, white wine and orange liqueur.
2 Whisk mixture together for 5 to 7 minutes, until it triples in volume and a ribbon forms when whisk is lifted out.
3 Remove pan from heat and continue whisking for 1 minute.
4 To serve, place fruit in 6 balloon wine glasses and spoon sabayon over fruit.

cold sabayon

1 cup	**whipping cream**	250 mL

1 Cool sabayon mixture in the bowl, whisking occasionally so that it holds its shape. When sabayon mixture has cooled completely, whip cream in a separate bowl until cream holds stiff peaks. Fold gently into sabayon.

2 Scrape sabayon into a glass bowl and chill until ready to serve. If mixture separates, whisk together again. The mixture will hold together for up to 3 days.
Serves 6

chocolate ginger bars

This easy bar recipe can be made by kids, but the flavour is definitely grown-up. Because it is rich, cut it into small pieces.

1/3 cup	**butter**	75 mL
8 oz	**semisweet chocolate**	250 g
3 tbsp	**corn syrup**	45 mL
8 oz	**ginger cookies**	250 g
2 tbsp	**icing sugar**	25 mL

1 In a medium pot, melt the butter, chocolate and corn syrup together over low heat, stirring occasionally.
2 Place the ginger cookies in a food processor or blender. Process into coarse crumbs (you should have about 2 cups/500 mL). Stir into the chocolate mixture.
3 Spread in a greased 8-inch (2 L) cake pan. Refrigerate for 2 hours. Cut into 2-inch (5 cm) squares, then cut each square in half. Dust with icing sugar. Remove from the pan. Place in small paper muffin cups. Store in the refrigerator.
Makes 32 bars

peanut butter melting moments

These rich, buttery cookies melt in your mouth.

1 cup	all-purpose flour	250 mL
½ cup	icing sugar	125 mL
¼ cup	cornstarch	50 mL
2 tsp	grated orange rind	10 mL
½ cup	butter	125 mL
¼ cup	peanut butter	50 mL

1 Preheat the oven to 300° F (150° C).
2 In a large bowl, mix together the flour, icing sugar, cornstarch and orange rind.
3 With a pastry blender or your fingers, blend in the butter and peanut butter until the mixture resembles coarse crumbs.
4 Gather the mixture into a ball. Pinch off small pieces and shape into 1-inch (2.5 cm) balls.
5 Place the balls on an ungreased baking sheet. Flatten the balls slightly, then mark them with the tines of a fork.
6 Bake for 20 to 25 minutes, or until lightly browned. Cool on a wire rack.
Makes about 24 cookies

caramel sauce

A quick sauce for ice cream, poached pears, chocolate cake or banana splits. The sauce can be made up to five days ahead.

½ cup	butter	125 mL
½ cup	firmly packed brown sugar	125 mL
½ cup	granulated sugar	125 mL
½ cup	whipping cream	125 mL
1 tsp	vanilla extract	5 mL

1 In a medium pot, combine all the ingredients except the vanilla. Heat to boiling over medium heat, stirring frequently. Boil and stir for 1 minute.
2 Cool slightly and stir in the vanilla. Store, covered, in the refrigerator. Reheat before serving.
Makes 2 cups (500 mL)

wicked chocolate mousse

This luxurious, dense mousse will keep for four or five days if you don't eat it first.

4 oz	semisweet chocolate or bittersweet chocolate	125 g
½ tsp	instant coffee powder	2 mL
½ cup	whipping cream	125 mL
1	egg, beaten	1
¼ tsp	vanilla extract	1 mL

1 Break up the chocolate and place in a pot with the coffee and cream. On low heat, slowly melt the chocolate, stirring until the mixture is smooth. Remove from the heat.
2 Stir in the egg and vanilla and beat together until slightly thickened. Pour into 4 individual serving dishes and chill.
Serves 4

There is no secret to getting the best-tasting chocolate cakes or cookies – it's all in the chocolate. If chocolate is good enough to eat, then it's good enough for cooking. I prefer the European bittersweet varieties, which pack the most flavour.

brie fondue

My daughter Katie whips this up for her friends. Brie melts well, and the brown sugar enhances the mellow taste. Make individual fondues in small soufflé dishes for a more formal dinner. Strawberries, pear or apple slices also make good dippers.

8 oz	Brie cheese	250 g
2 tbsp	brown sugar	25 mL
¼ cup	sliced almonds or walnuts	50 mL
	Fresh strawberries	
	Crackers	

1 Preheat the oven to 375° F (190° C).
2 Cut the Brie into pieces and remove the top rind. Pack into a small ovenproof dish.
3 Sprinkle on the brown sugar and almonds.
4 Bake for 8 to 10 minutes, or until the cheese melts.
5 Serve with strawberries or crackers to dip into the hot melted cheese.
Serves 4

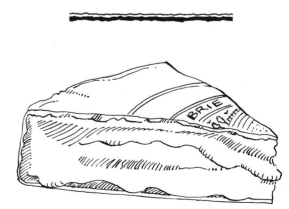

index

181

182

185

index

Photography credits

Douglas Bradshaw: Cream of sweet potato soup (food styling by Olga Truchan), Aromatic beef with pinot noir sauce (food styling by Olga Truchan), Rack of lamb provençale with garlic confit (food styling by Olga Truchan), Warm lentil salad with feta (food styling by Kate Bush), Linguine with seafood (food styling by Olga Truchan). **Ed O'Neill:** Do-it-yourself tostados (food styling by Kate Bush), Red snapper with lemon garlic butter (food styling by Karen Jull-O'Brien), Lemon-scented chicken (food styling by Kate Bush), Apple ginger crisp (food styling by Karen Jull-O'Brien), Derby squares (food styling by Kate Bush). **Vince Noguchi:** Bruschetta (food styling by Jennifer McLagan), Sabayon (food styling by Jennifer McLagan). **Michael Kohn:** Pork tenderloin with apples and brandy. **Michael Mahovlich:** Poached salmon fillets, Roasted red potatoes (food styling by Rosemarie Superville). **Robert Wigington:** Salad pizza (food styling by Kate Bush).

The following photographs and recipes are courtesy of LCBO's *Food & Drink* magazine: Cream of sweet potato soup, Aromatic beef with pinot noir sauce, Rack of lamb provençale with garlic confit, Pork tenderloin with apples and brandy, Roasted red potatoes, Sabayon, and Bruschetta.

Some of the recipes in this book originally appeared in *Toronto Life, Canadian Living, Canadian House and Home* and *Canadian Select Homes.*

Produced by Lorraine Greey Publications Limited
Editor: Shelley Tanaka
Cover illustration: Sally J.K. Davies
Text illustrations: Barbara Griffin
Author photograph: Greig Reekie